POSITIVE MIND THERAPY

POSITIVE MIND THERAPY
Lessons From Real Life

RAKESH K MITTAL

A Sterling Paperback

STERLING PAPERBACKS
An imprint of
Sterling Publishers (P) Ltd.
A-59, Okhla Industrial Area, Phase-II,
New Delhi-110020.
Tel: 26387070, 26386209; Fax: 91-11-26383788
E-mail: mail@sterlingpublishers.com
www.sterlingpublishers.com

POSITIVE MIND THERAPY
Lessons From Real Life
© Rakesh K Mittal
ISBN 978 81 207 2895 0
Reprint 2006, 2007, 2011

All rights are reserved.
No part of this publication may be reproduced, stored in a retrieval system or transmitted, in any form or by any means, mechanical, photocopying, recording or otherwise, without prior written permission of the original publisher.

Printed in India
Printed and Published by Sterling Publishers Pvt. Ltd.,
New Delhi-110 020.

This book is dedicated to all those persons and organisations which are selflessly engaged in the propogation of spiritual wisdom in order to make this world a better place to live.

FOREWORD

Someone has said that it is not great sorrow, disease or death which clouds over the sunshine of life but the little daily dyings. Therefore, if we properly handle our seemingly ordinary activities we would not only be winning the battle of this life but also that of the hereafter.

The narratives contained in the present collection of Shri R K Mittal relates to the everyday occurrences. He possesses the enviable faculties of keen observation, dispassionate analysis and clear expression. He has understood the mathematics of life and is able to cull the fundamental truths and lessons from the unfolding events and human behaviour.

The present achievement is not the first of its kind. He cultivated the quality of positive thinking as a basic ingredient of his *sadhana* and, as a result, was able to compile the *Dictionary of Positive Thoughts*. An optimist endeavours while a pessimist loses a battle before it begins. Shri Mittal has equipped himself well to derive positive lessons from life and has been able to place some of them before the seekers through his *Positive Mind Power*. These two brilliant collections are now supplemented by the present one. It is note worthy that Shri Mittal's observations are not only replete with practical wisdom but also bear the imprint of the Indian philosophy and way of life.

Fearlessness is a great virtue, but it can cause injury to oneself or injustice to others if it is not tempered with equipoise, kindness, forgiveness and humility. In chapter XVI of the Bhagavad Gita, divine virtues have been enumerated in the first three *shlokas*. Fearlessness comes first and humility comes at the other end. In between there are 24 other virtues. Shri Mittal has rightly come to the conclusion that fearlessness has to be cultivated along with compassion, justice, kindness, forgiveness, etc. In another chapter, he sees a silver lining in poverty also. It reminds me of a saint's wish :

सुख के माथे सिल परे नाम हिए ते जाय।
बलिहारी वा दुखः की पलपल नाम रटाय।।

Once we know ourselves — आत्मज्ञान — the mathematics of life — its alpha and omega — will reveal itself. When Shri Mittal says that one should live like an asymptote, he is in fact reminding us that we should live in this world in a dispassionate manner, following *Anaskta Karmayoga* and all the time remember the ultimate destination of the Self meeting the Universal Self. In the essay on the dialling code of God he again tells us that it is by overcoming ego, greed, passion, and anger that one qualifies oneself for liberation and the realisation of the Supreme Being.

Shri Mittal's background of science, particularly mathematics, and engineering, lends greater authority to his spiritual observations. I am confident that their study will prove most rewarding and beneficial.

2/5 Vishwas Khand **T P Tewary**
Gomti Nagar, Lucknow-226010 Former Chief Secretary,
Phone : 0522-2309662 Uttar Pradesh
Lt. Governor, Pondicherry

PREFACE

This book is in continuation of my previous book titled *Positive Mind Power*. In the preface of that book, I had mentioned my wish to share whatever I have learnt in life. This book is, perhaps, the result of the same resolve.

My contemplative nature has led me to draw deep lessons from the ordinary events of day-to-day life. With time, the nature of these lessons became more and more spiritual. Therefore, I had to debate mentally about the title of the present book. Positive lessons fitted the first set of lessons but I consider that this set of lessons should be called spiritual. Hence the present book is being titled as *Positive Mind Therapy*. I also feel that what is spiritual is also positive. After all, when we talk of spirituality, the expansion or vastness is automatically implied which can only be positive.

My long contemplation has given me the conviction that it is ultimately the spiritual dimension of life which makes a personality integrated in the true sense. Having achieved that, all the conflicts of life cease to upset us and we can dive in the ocean of this seemingly dangerous world like proficient divers. The purpose of this book is to pass on this conviction to those who may be in doubt, despite having achieved a lot in their lives. I present this collection in all humility with the hope that it will help them.

Once again, many have helped and inspired me in this work. Without naming anyone, I express my deep gratitude to all of them.

> There are two kinds of people in this world ....
> Givers and Takers !
> The Takers eat well ....
> but the Givers sleep well !

BENEDICTION

If one lives his life properly and well, it will inevitably take him more and more to the inner realms of himself as years pass by. And the habit of introspection will grow, leading him to greater inner worth and ability. Knowledge gained from the schools, colleges and other centres, relating as it does to the field of objects alone, is bound to remain inadequate and incomplete. Is there not a distinct part or facet of knowledge, relating specifically to the Subject, which is accessible only through one's own timely reflection and introspection?

The Subject-knowledge is even more extensive and deep. The first phase of it is revealed when the mind begins to yearn for qualities like confidence, tolerance and a sense of hope and assurance, despite all the troubles and torments one passes through. It is truly an art and virtue to remain unshaken in all circumstances, enriching oneself through every experience, interaction and event.

Rakesh Mittal is obviously one who belongs to this category of introspecting and self-enriching individuals. Placed in the field of public administration, he has a very responsible and busy life, having to meet a variety of people — both administrative and general public. Human relationship, as an art and refinement, has thus to feature prominently in his thoughts, conduct and movements.

In spite of frequent travels, change of functions and responsibilities, Rakesh keeps his routine of daily tennis and walk. The former, perhaps, tends to relax him, while the latter gives him an opportunity to look around, think and relate matters in a manner that stimulates contemplation. Many may share these habits and practices of his. But the one step beyond, namely, recording the thoughts and findings each time whenever something relatable transpires, is not so common a trait. Rakesh has happily a good measure of this additional note.

Thus he first collected the 'positive thoughts' of many thinkers and strung them together for release, as his first book. His interest grew into a pursuit resulting in the formulation of his own '*Positive Mind Therapy*', his second book. Now Rakesh is before his readers again with his latest introspection: "*Positive Mind Therapy*", a dimension every thinking individual should aspire for and achieve to make his life complete and fulfilling.

One's knowledge assumes spiritual dimension only when it begins to reveal to him the existence of the Spirit and its magnificence. Proper reflection will reveal that in one's actions and interactions, the Spirit, the Subject, alone exists in everything, everywhere and every time. The world of objects is quite imposing. But the fact remains that the entire objective existence owes itself unquestionably to the might and grandeur of the Subject alone.

Any action or experience can proceed only from the Subject to the object. To enable the process, the Subject and the object have to be distinct from each other. What is the Subject? It is not the mind or intelligence or even their further derivatives. Like the body and the objects surrounding it, all these have the status of mere object. That is why you say 'my mind, my intelligence'. The possessive case always denotes something different from you and objective to the 'I' in you. You are the undoubted Subject of all.

Like the reflective magnitude of the plane mirror, this Subject has infinite reflective, conceptual and cognitive dimensions. It reigns independent throughout. Being changeless and independent, it is the one Source of all, the Supreme Reality. Spiritual introspection, to be meaningful, has to take the thinker to this inward source, the Subject, the Ultimate Reality.

Spirituality is not a myth or a speculation, as perhaps religion is at times. It is, on the other hand, the most rational and experiential. Spiritual discussion leads man to his own inner depth and expanse, without which no one's life is worth living. Of the two regular states of awareness — namely the wakeful and deep sleep — the *sushupti* (sleep state) clearly gives evidence of the independent, ever present Subject, the Spirit. As a full contrast, it also proves the utterly changeful and dependent nature of all things in the world, including your body, mind and intelligence. Change disproves the real. Constancy, on the other hand, denotes the Supreme Reality without any doubt whatever. Decide now whether you will call all the objects including your body, mind and the rest 'unreal'.

I wish the readers of this book as well as its author adequate subjective spiritual strength and wisdom. May you all have unassailable confidence, clarity and stability. Be not swept or shaken by the undue power and influence of objects. Instead be graced every time by the splendour and magnificence of the one Subject, which everyone of you verily are.

Self-knowledge verily means freedom from the mind's shackles. Such freedom inevitably leads to inner composure, spiritual brilliance, and expansion of the heart and mind. When the seeker begins to revel in his inner delight, his mind's narrowness will give place to all folds of love and oneness. The enlightened hearts thus become sarva-bhota-hite-rattah - engaged in the welfare of all beings.

— **Swamiji**

CONTENTS

Foreword by T P Tewary   vii
Preface   ix
Benediction by Swami Bhoomananda Tirtha   xi

1. The State of Fearlessness   1
2. The Mathematics of Life   3
3. Living like an Asymptote   6
4. The Richness of Poverty   9
5. Fission of the Human Mind   11
6. Being like the Sea   14
7. Friends vs Relatives   16
8. Diving in the World Ocean   19
9. Four Dimensions of Personality   21
10. My Job is Very Important   25
11. Positive Revenge   28
12. Living as an Observer   30
13. Tenure on This Earth   33
14. Discovery of a Friend   35
15. A Total View of Life   38
16. Constructive Destruction   41
17. Silver Jubilee   43
18. False Ceiling   46
19. Permanent or Less Temporary   48
20. Minus Infinity to Plus Infinity   50
21. Varilux Lens   52

22.	Coordinates of Life	55
23.	Traffic Jam	58
24.	Ohm's Law of Life	61
25.	The Divine Court	64
26.	God as an Accountant	67
27.	When You keep Your Word	70
28.	Gandhiji's Monkey	73
29.	Inspiration from the Void	75
30.	The Fall of Shivalik	77
31.	Dialling Code of God	80
32.	From Known to Unknown	83
33.	Room for Improvement	86
34.	State of Flux	89
35.	Living in the Present	90
36.	Women and Gold	92
37.	Coconut Water	94
38.	Knowledge and Wisdom	95
39.	Life before Death	97
40.	Role of the Wicked	99
41.	All Things are Small	101
42.	Strength of Humility	103
43.	Power of Compassion	105
44.	Variety, not Hierarchy	107
45.	Answers of Our Problems	109
46.	The Entropy Law	111
47.	The Photograph has Changed	114
48.	Guru Poornima	116
49.	God and the Government	119
50.	Who Needs God	123
	The Goal of Life	

1
THE STATE OF FEARLESSNESS

I remember an incident in early 1979 when I was posted as additional district magistrate at Meerut. Once the commissioner of the Division visited the district and I accompanied him on his tour. The visit went off very well and he was quite happy with the work done. In the evening, we were returning in the same car on our way to Meerut. The Commissioner was a very good man and the success of the tour gave me some courage to speak frankly during the journey. At that time I was a young officer with only three years of service and was unaware of many realities of public administration. However, I was aware of the interference of vested interests in administration, as a result of which most officers were not able to work fearlessly. So I asked him certain questions about this aspect, curious to know whether it was possible for an honest and sincere civil servant to work fearlessly despite outside pressure. The answer was, naturally, not that simple but he said that though it was definitely possible to work fearlessly it required a lot of wisdom and other virtues like ability and perceptiveness, for an honest and sincere civil servant to reach that stage. The matter ended there but the question occupied my mind for a long time.

As far as I can introspect, I have always tried to work sincerely and honestly. I was not troubled by people who had vested interests, as most of the time I could get my way through them. Not only this, I have often been able to get their appreciation. But to say that I have reached a stage of total fearlessness is not correct. Therefore, the issue still occupies my mind as I wish to reach this state. In my subsequent years of public service, I constantly strived to reach that stage of fearlessness and the process is still on. I believe that a civil servant should not make mere survival his target though he must survive those people who cared for its purity and cleanliness. Let us hope that this balance will be maintained and the sarovar will continue to remain pure, thus serving the needs of well-wishers as well as neutralising the depredations by exploiters.

The Power of Perseverance

The heights
by great men
reached and kept ....

.... were not attained
by sudden flight,
But they, while their

companions slept ....
.... were toiling upwards
in the night.

2
THE MATHEMATICS OF LIFE

Mathematics has always been my best subject. I never scored less than ninety-five per cent marks in this subject and have notched hundred per cent many times. In my BSc examination, I scored 150 out of 150 marks, breaking all previous records. In engineering also, I was awarded the Cautley Memorial Gold Medal for mathematics for scoring the highest marks in this subject. In fact, good scores in mathematics always helped me greatly in my academic performance.

All this is not to highlight my personal achievement. The intention is altogether different but before coming to that, I would like to mention certain additional facts. The first is that this score was achieved effortlessly. The second is that I never studied the subject at the time of the examination. The third fact is that I studied only the book prescribed in the course. Lastly, there were some students in my class who were equally good in the subject, though I always scored the highest.

Now I come to the reason for this achievement. The first is that I always considered mathematics as a game which was a pleasure to play. It always gave me entertainment and refreshment instead of tiredness or boredom. Secondly, I paid maximum attention to understand the underlying principles of the subject. For example, in trigonometry, I understood the concepts of the Pythagoras' theorem and it always helped me in solving the problems. Similarly, in algebra, I mastered numbers and for calculus understood the very definition of differential coefficient well. By this process I found each branch of mathematics easy and I performed well in all of them. I am still able to recollect and apply these fundamentals whenever required. Thus, the secret of an effortless performance was a clear understanding of the fundamentals of the subject.

After finishing my engineering course, I worked for sometime in an engineering company before joining the Indian Administrative Service. I found this service satisfying, despite the odds of public life. My engineering background helped me to adopt an analytical approach to administration, and enabled me to perform quite well in the service. I feel that the mathematical approach helped me greatly in this achievement.

Having completed over twenty-five years of service and reaching the age when one should acquire enough wisdom to look at life in its true perspective, I feel that life is also like mathematics and the problems of life are similar to the problems of mathematics. If the fundamentals of life are understood, then life's problems can also be faced easily. In that case, life becomes a pleasure and its difficult problems only add to the pleasure of living. On the other hand, if the concepts of life are not clear, even routine problems of life disturb us and we make ourselves miserable.

Here I am not going into the details of the fundamentals of life. In brief, I would say that life is a wonderful opportunity for elevation and it should not be wasted on mundane affairs only, just as the purpose of mathematics is not merely to pass the examination but to understand and apply its principles in life. Similarly, the purpose of life should be understood in its true sense and it should be taken as an opportunity for achieving its goal. With that clarity in the mind, the difficulties attached to life become very small and add to the pleasure of living. Such people score high in the mathematics of life without much difficulty. In worldly terms, there may be more prosperous persons around them but when it comes to the examination of life, it is they who secure the highest marks. And all this happens effortlessly.

So let us first accept the simile of life with mathematics and feel the urge to understand its fundamentals. Once we have the urge, we will find the way and help will come from unexpected sources. No doubt, a sustained effort is required on our part, but once the process of understanding is over, life becomes scoring as well as enjoyable, like the subject of mathematics. We can then easily aim to score cent per cent marks, no matter how difficult the paper is. At least, I am striving to score cent per cent marks in the mathematics of life too.

You are at the top when ....

- You clearly understand.... that failure is an event, not a person.... that yesterday ended last night, and today is your brand new day.
- You have made friends with your past, are focused on the present, and optimistic about your future.
- You know that success doesn't make you, and failure doesn't break you.
- You are filled with faith, hope and love; and live without anger, greed, guilt, envy, or revenge.
- You have made friends of your adversaries, and have gained the love and respect of those who know you best.

3

LIVING LIKE AN ASYMPTOTE

The word 'asymptote' may appear strange to many, particularly to those who have not studied higher mathematics. Though the word finds a place in all English dictionaries, I feel it needs an explanation. To understand 'asymptote', one has to understand certain mathematical terms. First the term 'curve' is to be understood. It is a geometrical figure following a defined relationship in its two coordinates, a simple example of a curve being a circle. The second term to be understood is 'tangent'. It is a line which meets the curve only at one point. Normally a line intersects a curve at two or more points depending upon the shape of the curve, but when it intersects or meets only at one point, the same line becomes a tangent.

We have two types of curves. Some have a finite size while the others are infinite in size. The examples of finite size curves are a circle, an ellipse, etc., and the examples of infinite size curves are parabola, hyperbola, etc. Both types of curves have tangents. In fact, each point on the curve can have a tangent and these tangents follow certain mathematical rules. Of course, there are no such rules for lines which are not tangents.

Having understood this, the term 'asymptote' can also be explained. An 'asymptote' is a line which is just like a tangent but is not a tangent. This is so because the point of contact between an asymptote and the curve is at infinity. At infinity, the curve and the tangent merge into each other. Only a curve of infinite size can have an 'asymptote'. It is quite difficult to grasp the concept of contact at infinity as it is only creation of the imagination. 'Asymptotes' also follow certain mathematical laws.

I studied this concept about thirty years back and it fascinated me greatly. Generally, students found it too difficult to grasp, but those who understood its concept, found it easy. I shall now relate the concept of tangent and asymptote with life in order to make it easy and interesting.

The world we live in is like a limited size curve. A person living a worldly life is like a line which is a non-tangent. He has no rules to guide him and follows the path which suits him at a particular point of time. In other words, he lives a directionless life, resulting in frequent intersection with the worldly curve which may be compared to the clashes or conflicts he comes across in his worldly life. The answer to this lies in living a properly directed life so that life becomes a tangent to the world. It means that the contact with the world is reduced to just a point. Such a person has very few clashes or conflicts with the world and leads a smooth life with the right direction. Tangents at various points means that it is possible to live smoothly, if one wishes to.

Having achieved this stage, one can switch on to a higher state of living. For this, one has to enlarge one's vision to infinity. This is like shifting to infinite curves, from limited or finite curves. While one can draw tangents on each point here, an asymptote can also be drawn on such curves, meaning that while the line goes along the curve, it does not touch it at all, at least in the finite dimension. In terms of living, it is like living a life above the world. However, this is possible only when we have our vision focused on infinity and is not possible in the case of finite vision. In such a state, there is no clash with the world and one can be above it while living in it. It is like the movement of a hovercraft which is above the water despite being in it.

A comparison can also be drawn with the meeting or merger of an asymptote with the curve. As said earlier, this is possible at the infinite only. In terms of living it means that the ultimate aim of life is to achieve divinity, that is, to merge with the infinity. However, this is not possible as long as we identify ourselves only with the body and remain limited in our vision. As the bodily sense reduces, the vision gets widened. If the physical consciousness goes completely, the vision becomes infinite and a complete merger which is possible only after the body is gone, takes place. It is then like meeting or merging of an asymptote with the curve at infinite distance. This is, perhaps, the ultimate aim of living. The Creator or God can be compared with an infinite curve. Let us try to become its asymptote so that all along we are with it, and the gap narrows as we go through the path of life and ultimately merge into it when the body is totally gone.

Nothing in the world

can take the place of persistence!

Talent will not ... nothing is more common,

than unsuccessful men with talent.

Genius will not ...

unrewarded genius is almost a proverb.

Education will not ...

the world is full of educated derelicts.

Persistence and determination alone

are amnipotent !

President Calvin Collidge

4
THE RICHNESS OF POVERTY

Over the past few years, television has made tremendous progress in our country. Not only has the number of programmes increased manifold, but the quality too has improved greatly. The competition between various channels has also contributed to the improvement. There is such a bewildering variety and number of programmes that it is difficult to decide what to see. However, some of the programmes are really good and have given useful messages to the viewers. Two serials from which I drew important messages are *Nukkad* and *Junoon*, messages which I would like to share.

The serial *Nukkad* was on the life in a street corner of a small town. All the characters of the serial were persons who could barely make their living. Some were not even employed and depended on the help of their colleagues. Some had developed the habit of drinking due to frustration. They were, at times, also exploited by vested interests. Overall, they were miserable people and had no apparent joy in their lives.

On the other hand, *Junoon* was a story of very rich people who had accumulated their lakhs of rupees by dubious means. Many of them were engaged in underworld activities and had intense rivalries with each other. Outwardly they displayed affluence and moved around in the upper class of society. But inwardly, they too were frustrated, and often resorted to drinking as a result thereof.

When we look at these two groups of people, some interesting observations can be made. In *Nukkad*, the group as a whole appears quite cheerful and contented. They enjoy every moment of life despite all the problems they face. They try to help each other beyond their means. They happily accept the shortcomings of each other and genuinely try to help. There is no tension visible on their faces. Overall, the group, though beset by problems, is quite happy and enjoys life to the extent possible under the circumstances.

The opposite is the case in the serial *Junoon*. In this group, the characters are so busy amassing wealth that they have no time to enjoy life. The unfair, illegal means of making a fortune further adds to their worries. Not only this, they are always fearful of the police or of a rival or of their own men. This makes their lives very tense, rendering it totally joyless. Almost all of them have great tension in their family lives too.

This made me think about the very definition of richness or poverty. I feel these are not at all absolute terms but simply the states of mind. I find it difficult to say which of the two groups is richer. If one is richer outwardly, it is very poor inwardly and vice versa. The first group, despite being poor, is happy, while the second group is miserable despite all the riches. And if we go by the ultimate aim of living, which is happiness, it is the first group which achieves the objective and not the latter.

I do not intend to arrive at any absolute conclusion. I am just raising a question for those who feel that happiness lies only in having more and more riches, irrespective of the means of acquiring them. I am also not saying that happiness lies in poverty. Perhaps, the reality is somewhere in between. For true happiness there has to be a balance between the outer and the inner growth. In the examples cited, the happiness of the first group as well as the misery of the second group are both the results of their ignorance. But I feel that bliss, even if out of ignorance, is better than misery of any kind. From this point of view, the state of poverty has more richness.

❈

5
FISSION OF THE HUMAN MIND

As economic development progresses, the consumption of energy is also increasing at a fast rate. As a result, man is engaged in exploring new sources of energy. The use of atomic energy for the generation of power has given some relief though it has serious environmental problems. However, since it can solve the problem of the energy crisis to a great extent, the subject of atomic energy becomes important for all.

When my son was preparing for the class X examination, I guided him in science. When I went through the chapter on atomic energy, I found it very interesting and drew some very interesting lessons from it. This is what I am going to share here.

Here, some background of the concept of atomic energy is required. An atom consists of three basic particles, namely, protons, neutrons and electrons. The protons and neutrons are located in the nucleus and the electrons revolve around the nucleus in different orbits. A large amount of energy is released when the nucleus of a heavy atom is broken into two or more smaller nuclei. Similarly, when the nuclei of two or more lighter atoms are made to merge into each other, resulting in a heavier nucleus, then also a large amount of energy is released. The former is known as Nuclear Fission and the latter is known as Nuclear Fusion. Such reactions take place under certain special conditions. If we are able to create these conditions, the reaction can take place on a large scale also. The energy, thus released, is known as atomic energy. If controlled, this energy can be used for running a power plant and if not, the same energy can turn into an atom bomb.

So far, the control of the reaction has been possible in fission and not in fusion. The fuel or the radioactive substance commonly used in fission is uranium. When the nucleus of uranium is bombarded by a neutron, it breaks into two smaller nuclei and simultaneously, three neutrons accompanied with a large amount of energy are produced. These three neutrons again bombard three other nuclei of uranium and the process is repeated again and again. If the number of neutrons bombarding the uranium nuclei is controlled, we get energy at a constant rate which can be used for good purposes, otherwise the same device can have a disastrous effect in the form of a bomb. The control of the reaction is done by controlling the speed and the number of neutrons and for this we use a moderator and controlling rods in the reactor. When the reaction is in total control, the energy is released at a constant rate and can be used for power generation.

I shall now compare this phenomenon with the human mind. The human mind is also like a radioactive substance which keeps on emitting various thoughts. The thoughts are of various kinds but we can classify them in two categories. Some thoughts are active in nature while the others are passive. Active thoughts make the mind act and in the process, the power of the mind is made use of. Such thoughts may be called desires. Passive thoughts, on the other hand, do not make the mind act, but are simply observed by the mind . Thus active thoughts or desires can be compared with moving particles like neutrons, protons, etc., and the mind with a heavy radioactive nucleus, like uranium. When active thoughts strike it, tremendous energy is emitted by the mind like that in Nuclear Fission. However, to make good use of this power, certain conditions similar to those in a nuclear reactor should exist.

First of all, we should have a neutral attitude towards desires like the neutrality of a neutron. It means that an attitude of detachment should be developed towards our desires. It does not mean that desires should be absent but that they should be controlled. Only the neutral or detached thoughts are in a position to make the best use of our tremendous mental energy.

Secondly, the speed of a neutron has to be at its optimum level. Either too much or too little will lead to no action. In the same way, active thoughts should neither be very fast nor very slow. That is to say, that moderation is required in our thinking so that our thoughts are able to tap the maximum energy of the mind which exists in abundance. This condition suggests that our lifestyle should be moderate in order to make the maximum use of our power.

The third condition is also very important. In a nuclear reactor, each neutron gives rise to three neutrons which have to be controlled after a point. The human mind also generates more and more desires which then strike the mind harder and make it release more power. Up to an extent, this increase is healthy because the mind's potential is used in a positive manner. However, beyond a point, the generation of more desires becomes destructive. Therefore, it is necessary to absorb or control these additional desires to make the best use of the mind, very much like controlling the number of neutrons in the reactor.

Thus, detachment, moderation and regulation are three essential conditions for making the best use of our mind power. If any one of these is missing, the mind's power will either remain unused or will become destructive. How to achieve these conditions is not the subject here but achieving them is certainly possible. It is up to us to use the mind either as a 'Power Plant' or as an 'Atom Bomb'.

- Mind can make a hell of heaven or a heaven of hell.
- The human mind is like a parachute, it only works when it is open.

6
BEING LIKE THE SEA

Once I stayed in Madras for about a week with my family. We stayed in a guest house located on a beach near the sea, which added to the charm and pleasure of staying there. We had very pleasant morning walks along the mighty, surging sea, and its vastness touched our hearts. During our stay, I contemplated deeply on the nature of the sea and how it helps us to develop our own personality.

The first great quality of the sea is its vastness. It is so vast that the other shore of the sea is never seen by an ordinary person. We require magnitude in our personality too. Our vision should enlarge with our physical growth so that our personality becomes pleasant. An ordinary person may not think beyond himself, his family or a close social circle. Such vision needs further expansion and one should ultimately think of the whole creation. With such a vast vision, we start loving the whole creation of God and there is no room for lower tendencies like hatred, anger and jealousy.

The second quality of the sea is its depth. The vastness of the sea would be meaningless without its depth for this quality enables the sea to gain stability. Similarly, for the true development of our personality vast mundane knowledge is not sufficient as it may not give depth to our personality. This depth is acquired by developing wisdom which gives stability to our personality.

The third quality to be learnt from the sea is 'absorption'. It absorbs whatever is merged into it. All mighty rivers ultimately merge into the sea and it accepts all of them. Not only this, these rivers carry away with them all the filth created by human beings. The sea accepts that too. In turn it returns pure rain-water, retaining all the dirty water received by it. The sea water itself remains saltish though it is the ultimate source of all sweet water. This amounts to returning goodness in exchange for evil, a quality which should be part of the personality also, giving us mercy, kindness and compassion.

The last quality is 'stability' which can also be learnt from the sea. The sea level remains stable though universal forces cause some ups and downs in it periodically. That is why the mean sea level is a standard benchmark and does not change with time. Similarly, our mental variations as a result of interaction with the world should also be to the minimum and the effort should be to maintain it at the same level. This little variation of sea level only indicates that as long as we live in the world, absolute calmness may not be possible. That state can be achieved only when we firmly control our reactions and responses, both mentally and physically. However, while living in the world, stability can be maintained and the variation can be reduced to the minimum. This is the quality which brings serenity to our personality.

Thus four qualities of the sea, namely, vastness, depth, absorption, and stability are to be adopted in our personality. If we can do so, we may be as useful for the society as the sea is to the entire creation on the earth.

- For the good of many, for the happiness of many, great souled men take their birth.
- Tolerance is the only test of civilisation.

7
FRIENDS VS RELATIVES

'God gives us relatives. Thank God, we can choose our friends.' This is a thought I came across somewhere and have found useful. Many of us feel the difference between friends and relatives. At times, I have myself faced agony on account of several relatives but I have no complaint against them and accept the reality of their attitudes and shortcomings with grace. Such experiences in turn made me contemplate on the subject and I would like to share my thoughts.

To begin with, we must accept that every friend is also a relative of many others. Then how is it that as a friend, we find no problem with him while as a relative it would be a different story ? Obviously it must be the difference in the attitude of the observer. If, somehow, one is able to develop the same attitude towards both relatives and friends, the problem will disappear. It may be difficult to do so but it is definitely possible. To understand the situation better, let us look at the reasons for this difference.

The first reason is that we watch our relatives so closely that their weaknesses are known to us. After all, no one is perfect and even a very good person may have some shortcomings. Most of us have the tendency to dwell upon the faults of others. This tendency quite often shadows the good qualities of the person and we develop a bias.

The second reason is that relatives like brothers, sisters, uncles, and nephews grow together from childhood. They normally begin their relationships with the same status, but as time goes on, this status changes and quite often there is a wide gap between two relatives who were once at a similar stage, be it financial or social. This difference creates a feeling of jealousy and gives rise to the tendency to find fault with each other.

The third reason is undue expectation. Frequently, we are disappointed when we expect too much from others or have unrealistic expectations. Most of us feel that it is the duty of our relatives to help us, irrespective of whether we deserve it or not. Also, we do not even consider it necessary to appreciate and express our appreciation for the help extended by them, taking it for granted. We all like to be appreciated. At times help is not possible despite best efforts but the efforts made should also be appreciated. Instead of doing that, one tends to put the blame on the person who made the efforts and, naturally, this creates disharmony.

The fourth factor which is quite important is the age difference. We have no control on the timings of our physical birth. As we grow in age, we acquire wisdom. Most of us believe that wisdom and age are synonymous while this is not necessarily true. A young person may be wiser than an elderly one but those who do not believe that this is possible, find it difficult to accept any advice from younger people. Apart from this, at times they exploit the young on the basis of the age difference, showing contempt or scorn. The young may show patience up to a point, but if the limits are crossed, disharmony is created.

The fifth reason is the fact that once a blood relationship is created, it remains for as long as we live, though it may not have any meaningful purpose. It is not in our hands to cancel it out. While there are legal provisions to nullify a close relationship, such as a marital one, there is no such provision in the case of blood relations. Such relations can be terminated only at a mental and, perhaps, emotional level, but often it is not possible and the result is disharmony.

Having analysed the main reasons for the disparity in our attitudes towards friends and relatives, it is easy to understand why we have more harmony with our friends as compared to relations. Without going into the details again, it can be said that in the case of friends, we have a choice, we do not watch them very closely, we accept the difference in status, if any, we do not have any undue expectation, we do not take the age difference that seriously and we have the choice of terminating friendship rather easily. It may be clarified that here we are talking about good friends, otherwise the chances of disharmony between those who are only so-called friends are even greater.

The message is that it is the attitudes which create disharmony and not persons as such. The need is to change them and if positive attitudes are adopted, there will be no cause for disharmony even with relatives. Wise people advise treating even a grown-up son as a friend. The same is true for a husband or wife as it is equally true for other relatives. Once we remove the possible causes of disharmony, we can have friendly relations with all.

EXPECTATION

- An ounce without expectation is more than a pound with expectation.

- If you get attached, you become miserable.

- Life is a mirror and will reflect to the thinker what he thinks into it.

8

DIVING IN THE WORLD OCEAN

My wish to visit the Bombay High oil drilling site was granted in April 1995. The drilling site is located about 200 km away from the seashore and it takes almost an hour to reach there by a helicopter. The visit was well arranged and I enjoyed it immensely.

From the engineering point of view, the whole operation is amazing. The fixation of the drilling rigs and platforms is an engineering feat. The foundations of these structures are very deep in order to keep them stable. During the visit I met some engineers who had worked there in the initial days of construction and they narrated their experiences with great pride, expressing the thrill of achievement. They also told me that the foundation construction of these structures was the most difficult stage and to carry out this task, expert divers were called from other countries. Subsequently, the art of diving has been sufficiently developed in India too.

We also discussed the techniques of diving. I was told that deep-sea diving was a difficult job and a good amount of training was required for it. As the pressure of water increases when the diver goes down into the depths of the sea, he has to take measures to withstand the stress. The deeper the diver goes, the greater is the pressure. In earlier days, the training process took a long time as the divers were subjected to gradually increasing pressure before they could venture deep into the sea. Now, there are special equipments which create sea conditions artificially and the process of training is expedited. However, the principle of training remains the same, which is to create enough internal resistance or pressure to withstand the external pressure. If the diver does not do this, his body could collapse. I have drawn some very interesting inferences from this fact.

The world we live in is also like a sea. The deeper we go into it, the greater are the disturbing forces we have to face. If we are not trained or used to bear these pressures, we collapse and fail to achieve the goal of our existence. In that case, we sink and then blame the world for it. We forget the nature of the world and the fact that there is no use blaming external circumstances. We should, on the other hand, train ourselves to withstand the pressures of the world. For this, we have to develop enough internal strength so that the two neutralise each other and we are able to dive into this worldly sea like professional divers. If we remember this, we shall not only perform our roles well but will enjoy life too.

What does this mean in real life ? It means that one's development should be integrated. While it is desirable to have external growth, it may turn out to be disastrous if it is not matched by a corresponding internal growth. The greater the external growth, the greater is the need for internal growth too. That is why people with high positions, greater riches, greater fame, or power should be much more balanced than ordinary persons. If they are not so, the outer trappings may become the cause of their disaster.

The conclusion is that a balanced growth of personality makes us good divers, plunging confidently into this worldly sea. The world will then cease to be a source of danger or trouble for us and we can enjoy living in it, as well as perform our duties well.

- A man of wisdom lives in the world but the world does not live in him.
- How things look on the outside of us depends on how things are on the inside of us.

9

FOUR DIMENSIONS OF PERSONALITY

In February 1995, when our Spiritual Master graced our home at Calcutta, he spoke on the subject of "Spiritual Dimension of Personality". In the gathering, there were people from different walks of life. Due to his clarity of thought and skill of expression, the talk was of great help and significance and all of us listened to him with rapt attention. Swamiji built up the talk gradually, making the message more interesting and effective. Here is a summary of his talk, as I interpreted it in my own way.

'Personality' is a commonly talked about term and we all want to develop our own personalities. We must, therefore, first understand the term itself. Often we talk of a total or integrated personality, and this shows that personality has more than one component. Only when all the components are adequately developed, does the personality become total or integrated. What are these components and what are the characteristics attached to them? We shall use the word 'dimension' in place of 'component' in order to give it a larger scope.

The first dimension of our personality is 'physical'. It relates to our body, state of health, appearance, etc. Though this dimension is very important, we have little control over it. By and large the shape, size and the colour of our body is determined by our genes. The only thing in our hands is to maintain it well in order to remain healthy. For this, certain discipline is required in our habits. If we cultivate good habits, the body becomes an asset and the development of other dimensions of the personality becomes easier. For example, early rising and early to bed, simple food, regular exercises and cleanliness are habits which keep our bodies healthy. A healthy body generally also means a healthy mind. If the body gives trouble, it becomes difficult to concentrate on other things. Therefore, the development of other dimensions of the personality is also dependent on this dimension which may become less important once the other dimensions develop.

The second dimension of our personality is 'mental'. It relates to the mind which is superior to the body. Thus, this dimension of the personality is superior to the first one. It is the mind which works behind our sense organs. The eye cannot see if the mind refuses to accept the signals and so is the case with other sense organs. Similarly, the mind is capable of making our sense organs indulge in right or wrong activities. Thus, proper development of the 'mental dimension' is very important for using the powers of the physical body. It is the mind which makes us educated, skilled in our jobs and enthusiastic about our progress. Those who apply their minds in the right direction, achieve success in their goals. Some of us become doctors, engineers, businessmen or administrators according to our mental make-up. It is mainly the mental dimension which gives us the capacity to take care of our physical needs. But to say that personality development stops here is not correct. We have to add something more to our personality in order to make it integrated and this takes us to the third dimension.

Before we come to the third dimension, some elaboration is necessary. We all know that certain doctors are very kind, sympathetic and helpful while others are not so. It may be that someone in the latter category is more competent professionally but in terms of personality, the compassionate doctor is always considered to be better. The same goes for other professions also. We always prefer a person who is good, kind, helpful, and courteous even if those who are not so, are mentally or professionally more competent. This establishes the fact that there is a superior dimension of personality over the mental one.

This dimension is known as 'intellectual'. As said earlier, the mind, though superior to the sense organs, is capable of playing mischief if not controlled by a superior faculty. This faculty is called the 'intellect'. It is the intellect which gives us the wisdom to discriminate between good and bad. Obviously a person with such wisdom has a better personality compared to a person which makes us capable of better judgement and, therefore, useful, also for the society at large. In the process we earn respect and are considered to be good.

To add perfection to our personality, some finer qualities have to be acquired, even by good persons who may also suffer if they do not strive for them. This dimension of the personality is the 'Spiritual' one, the highest dimension. It is a fact that the world we live in is transitory. Even our good deeds are forgotten with time. Therefore, there is a need to transcend them too. If we do not do so, the same goodness may become a cause of misery. Also, goodness is only a relative term and its perception varies with persons and time. We do not get the same response from all persons, even for our good behaviour or virtues. Therefore, a sense of detachment has to be developed towards our good qualities too. It has been seen that many good and successful persons suffer just because they lack this aspect of the personality. One has to accept that all our actions are only a means to an end and the end is self-realisation. Those who understand this reality, develop the spiritual dimension at the right time and are fully prepared for all the eventualities of life. This dimension is thus superior to the earlier three dimensions and is necessary for the complete integration of the personality.

The idea, without going into more details, is to convey that for an integrated personality, all dimensions are necessary. They, of course, generally follow the order in which they have been described. I consider those four aspects like the four legs of a table which give it stability. Though a table with three or less number of legs may appear to be stable, any push or pressure will destabilise it. Similarly, a person with any of the dimensions missing may appear to be stable but is vulnerable to any accident in life which may disturb his equilibrium.

> - Humility, love, tolerance, mercy, are the true characteristics of a personality.
> - Personality is to man what perfume is to a flower.

10
MY JOB IS VERY IMPORTANT

Steel is an essential input in the economic development of any country, its consumption being an important parameter of progress. After independence, top priority was given to the steel industry, in which Jawaharlal Nehru took a special interest. As a result, many integrated steel plants were set up with the help of several developed countries.

Despite a good beginning, the steel industry in India did not develop as fast as it should have. While India and China began at the same level, today China is far ahead of us as are many other countries. There are several reasons for such a situation but one important reason is our general lack of pride in our work. It was also felt that the government's monopoly of all developmental activities has also been a cause, bringing about a major policy change which encouraged more private investment in developmental activities. The result of this change is yet to be seen fully but the initial response is heartening. This change in policy has also encouraged the public sector to perform better.

Steel production in India is still dominated by the public sector, though the position is changing gradually. New investment in steel is now mostly in the private sector. The public sector production has to improve mainly by way of more efficient working and modernisation, but fortunately, the response of the public sector in steel has been very encouraging in the new situation, giving rise to healthy competition between various plants. Some years ago, the prime minister had introduced an award for the best integrated steel plant in the country and the first award for the year 1992-93 went to a public sector unit, the Bhilai steel plant. I got an opportunity to visit this plant in July 1995. I noticed that the achievement of winning the prime minister's trophy was a matter of pride for everyone working in the plant. During a discussion with the management, I was told that the credit went to their workers and officers as they were a motivated lot and always worked to perform better. The results of the year 1993-94 and 1994-95 supported this statement.

I also learnt that the plant has been performing well on account of several factors, the most prominent being the strong work culture. There was a sense of pride in the job and that made all the difference. This reminded me of my meeting with a service manager of British Gas in the year 1990. At that time I was in the UK to attend a course on 'Public Enterprises Management'. During this course, we were taken to the British Gas Company office for a visit. It was a service branch and its main function was to take care of the complaints of the customers, a job which was being done quite efficiently, galvanised as it was by an elaborate incentive system introduced to reward efficiency. The most impressive part was the pride glowing on the faces of everyone. I still remember the beaming face of the service manager while explaining the importance of his job which was linked with consumer satisfaction. The spirit with which he worked was praiseworthy and the result was that everyone in the office was a satisfied person, and encouraged to do even better.

The message is that our attitude towards our job or work should change. For most of us, our job remains the same, whether we join it by choice or by the force of circumstances. For most of us a change is either not possible or is not in our hands. Since we spend a good amount of time on our job, we ought to develop a positive attitude towards it. Otherwise, it adversely affects our life and the result is unhappiness. A sense of pride should be developed towards it. The society needs the services of all and we play a complementary role to each other. Everyone is important at his place as even the highest cannot exist without the low. While the aim should be to strive towards high positions, no purpose is served if we keep grieving about being in a lowly position. In that case we downgrade ourselves and others also treat us as such. Instead we can turn even the so-called lower jobs into important ones by changing our attitude towards it. Srimad Bhagavad Gita, in its chapter on *Karma Yoga* says:

"Better one's 'duty', though devoid of merit, then the 'duty' of another well-discharged. Better is death in one's own duty; the 'duty' of another is fraught with fear" (3/35).

If all of us accept the importance of our duty and perform it well, the world will change so much for the better that there will be no cause for any grievance.

The Warmth of Compassion

A House is built
by hands .....

.... but a Home is built
by hearts !

You can live
without something ....

.... if you have
someone to live for !

11
POSITIVE REVENGE

Akbar was the greatest Mughal emperor and ruled over India during the sixteenth century (1556-1605). He is known for his liberal approach towards religion and for his competence in administration. He had a team of nine competent ministers called *navaratnas* (Nine Jewels), who looked after various departments of his administration. One of these *navaratnas* was Raja Birbal, a very interesting personality. In addition to helping the emperor in administrative matters, he also entertained him by his intelligence and wit. The emperor would often test the intelligence of his minister by asking him some seemingly strange questions which were always answered cleverly. Such dialogues between them are famous even today and are read with a lot of interest.

Once Akbar drew a straight line on a piece of paper and asked Birbal to shorten it without erasing any part of it. Birbal contemplated for a minute and then drew a longer line by its side. The line drawn by the emperor thus became shorter without being erased. The emperor and everyone in the court were greatly pleased and amused to see how Birbal had tackled the problem. The matter ended there. I have viewed this incident with philosophical interest and have drawn an important lesson from it.

The approach adopted by Birbal indicates a very positive approach. It can be compared with taking revenge without violence. In real life we come across many situations which have to be overcome without hurting anyone, including ourselves. Someone may have insulted us or hurt us, or some problem may be troubling us. A common man's approach may be either to suffer silently or to react destructively. This helps no one, least of all the person himself. When we think of destroying someone, we create negative impulses and in the process, harm ourselves.

Creative energy is thus wasted in destruction. The same situation can be dealt with in just the opposite manner. Instead of spending our energy in destruction, we may utilise it in construction. By adopting this approach, we raise ourselves above the person or the situation which has been troubling us. This automatically dwarfs them and in the process makes us bigger. From a worldly point of view, this may be called revenge on the person or the situation which troubled us.

Instances abound of greatness being the result when a person or situation has hurt someone. Gandhiji had to face humiliation from time to time and that made him more determined to secure Independence. Vivekananda passed through a phase of stark poverty and that made him so rich spiritually that he spread the message all over the world, calling upon people to eradicate poverty in order to be truly religious. Jamshedji Tata found no decent place in Mumbai to stay in when he decided to build the Taj Mahal Hotel there. Raja Ram Mohan Roy took a vow to fight against the 'Sati' system when he saw his sister-in-law being forced to burn in the funeral pyre of her husband. After facing humiliation and destruction in the Second World War, the Japanese constructed a new nation with greater determination and surpassed even the nations which caused them such humiliation and destruction. All these examples show that people did not surrender or act in a violent manner when a person or situation upset them. They overcame them constructively and in the process raised themselves above the person and the situation.
This is what Birbal also did while drawing a longer line in order to shorten a line already drawn. He did not erase it but dwarfed it. That is also a kind of revenge but a positive one.

12

LIVING AS AN OBSERVER

The central message of the Gita is that we should live in this world like an observer and perform our duties in a detached manner. Almost the same message is given by other religious scriptures also. It is said that all our pleasures and pains are the results of our attachment to our karmas. If we detach ourselves from our karmas, we free ourselves from their effect. Then we achieve harmony in life and are able to face all situations gracefully.

All this seems simple but is difficult in practice. For most of us, even the suggestion that we should rise above pleasure and pain seems strange. We may at best understand the need to rise above pain but not pleasure. We forget that pleasure and pain are two sides of the same coin and both have to coexist. The exclusion of only one is not possible and we have either to accept both of them or to accept none. Rising above both is a state of mind which gives us eternal joy and makes our life happy in the true sense. Such a state can be achieved only when we perform our Karma in a detached manner for the sake of our duty. We then live in the world like an observer.

I realised this fact when I was appointed as an observer by the Election Commission of India during the 1991 assembly elections of Uttar Pradesh. I was on duty in one of the most tension-ridden districts because the chief minister at that time was contesting from there. Some officers had avoided the observer's duty in that district and I was also advised to do the same by my well-wishers.

But after some contemplation, I decided to accept the appointment and to perform to the best of my capability. I thought that, after all, I was to act as an observer and my job was only to observe and report. The instructions issued by the Election Commission to the observers clearly mentioned that at best they could advise the district authorities, if the situation demanded it. The discretion of acting on such advice lay with the district authorities only. However, the observers were free to report their observations to the Election Commission, which in turn, took appropriate decisions.

My thoughts made my mind clear and I performed my duty not only fearlessly but also with a peaceful mind. As expected, the election in the district was full of problems. There were incidents of booth-capturing, snatching of ballot-papers and then killings. I observed them in an objective manner without being mentally affected by them. I reported my observations to the commission soon after the election process was over and, finally, the election was countermanded. Here the outcome was not so important as the state of mind I retained during the time. Subsequently, I was congratulated by my friends for performing a difficult task well.

A similar job was given to me by the Election Commission in November 1993 during the Himachal Pradesh assembly elections. It was a very peaceful election and there was not a single untoward incident. I enjoyed my job which took me to some remote villages of the state and gave an opportunity to mix with the native people. I also saw some of the most beautiful scenic spots of Himachal Pradesh.

I was again posted as an observer in the assembly election of Bihar in March 1995. This duty was also considered difficult. Firstly, there was so much uncertainty about the schedule of the elections that proper planning of the visits became difficult. Secondly, there was apprehension about the fairness of the elections and, thirdly, the infrastructure in the state was so poor that it became difficult to cover the whole area satisfactorily. I maintained the same attitude towards this task also and performed it in a very objective manner. Fortunately, my district was relatively peaceful and the district administration was alert. So everything went on well and I enjoyed my duty despite a hectic travel schedule. Again, the cause of the enjoyment was the fact that I was an observer and thus detached from the actions involved in the election process.

If we adopt a similar attitude in all our actions, they cease to bind us and we rise above both pleasure and pain. Life becomes enriching and its purpose is then achieved. Thus, living as an observer is the answer to all our problems.

> Qualities of a Karma Yogi — a divine worker, on enlightened man-of-action — are emphasized in Gita. These are : absence of ego, jealousy, self-interest and attachment to fruits of work; as also presence of equanimity, self-discipline spirit of sacrifice and awareness of God's omnipresence.
>
> **From : Yoga of Work**

13
TENURE ON THIS EARTH

Dr Dharma Vira an ICS officer was known for his competence and integrity. He once occupied the highest office of the Cabinet secretary in the Government of India. Thereafter, he served as governor of West Bengal and Karnataka. For a long time he was the chairman of the board of governors of the Administrative Staff College of India, Hyderabad. Everywhere he displayed both qualities in ample measure.

When Dr Dharma Vira entered his nineties, he issued an appeal to the national leaders and thinkers, suggesting certain measures in the interest of the nation. I also received a copy of the appeal and a phrase in this caught my attention. He had started with the sentence: 'I have now entered the 90th year of my life and it also indicates nearness to my tenure on this earth.' For civil servants, the word 'tenure' is a familiar term and they often talk about the tenure on a particular assignment. However, the phrase 'tenure on this earth' is something which is applicable to all of us and I am going to elaborate upon it here.

Civil servants are often transferred from one post to another. They also go on deputation to a particular organisation or to a Government of India post. Also, the nature of their jobs varies so widely that they generally do not get attached to a particular job or place. This helps them greatly in maintaining their objectivity, enabling them to deal with a situation or person in a fair manner. Perhaps, the objective behind transfers is mainly this.

The same is the case with a deputation. A civil servant goes on a deputation for a fixed tenure after which he reverts to his parent organisation. In the case of the Indian Administrative Service, the rules regarding a tenure are quite stringent, and an officer usually does not get even a day's extension. After the completion of a tenure, they revert back to their state cadre. They can again come on deputation after a fixed period known as the cooling period.

Officers aware of this reality do not get attached to their job and work with fairness and firmness. They gladly go back to their original places after the completion of their tenure. They do not think of an extension and make no efforts for it. But those who seek an extension face many problems. At times they compromise on their principles and face disgrace. They forget the fact that even the extended period comes to an end and their problems are only postponed. Of course, there may be exceptional situations where an extension may have to be sought or accepted for larger interests, personal or public.

Similar to an officer's tenure is our life on this earth. We know that it has to come to an end one day. The only difference is that we are not aware of the length of our tenure, though it is also said to be fixed by destiny. Since this is so, we should live on this earth in the spirit of acceptance. Getting attached to earthly things will add to our pain at the time of transfer or reversion from here. If we live in a detached manner, we shall not only be able to live gracefully but also to leave gracefully. This is what is expected of a civil servant on a tenure posting and from all of us during our "tenure on the earth".

- Short as life is, we make it still shorter by the careless waste of time.
- That it will never come again is what makes life so sweet.

14

DISCOVERY OF A FRIEND

There is a saying, 'In prosperity your friends know you and in adversity you know your friends'. It means that the attitudes of our so-called friends change when we are in trouble. All of us experience this reality some time or the other. If we analyse this in detail, we can prepare ourselves to face the situation in a dignified manner, without getting shocked when it happens.

We have to accept the fact that one cannot pick a friend, or purchase a friend, or compel anyone to be a friend. A true friend has to be discovered. In our good times there is no dearth of superficial friends, while true friends may get distanced or even lost. In our ignorance we fail to distinguish between them and consider the former as true friends. The mistake is realised when we face trouble. By that time it may be too late and our true friends may not return to us. The purpose of this analysis is to avoid such a situation.

Friends can be divided into four categories and the distinction is visible only during trouble. In good times it may not be possible to realise the distinction. Conversely, a false friend may appear more dear. We shall now describe these categories of friends.

The first category of friends can be called 'Rejoicers'. They not only rejoice or, rather, exploit our good days but also silently rejoice at our bad days. Outwardly they may show false grief in our trouble and if it persists and they see no early possibility of its going, they leave us like rats on a sinking ship. It would be no surprise if they also mutter the words, "Good, it happened to you". This is the worst category of friends and in a sense, they are worse than an enemy. We must be careful about such friends right from the beginning as they often prove to be harmful.

The second category of friends are called 'Sympathisers'. They are better than the first category. Such friends show sympathy in our trouble but do nothing beyond that. Secretly, they feel relieved, thinking, "Thank God, it did not happen to us." If the trouble persists, they gradually distance themselves and disappear in due course. We may at best call them harmless friends. We need not be unduly concerned or upset about them and should accept their attitude as the way of the world.

The third category of friends can be called 'Helpers'. In practical life this is the best category of friends and they may be called friends in the true sense. They are truly pained by our trouble and try to help us. They genuinely ask the question, "Why did it happen to you?" This is the category of friends we discover during our bad days. We can share our problems with them and also ask for their help, if required. Of course, we should not expect too much from them and only reasonable help should be asked for. It is also seen that many of such friends are those whom we do not consider so close during our good days.

The last category of friends is very rare. We may call this category the 'Sacrificers'. They are prepared to make any sacrifice for a friend in trouble. They ask the question, "Why did it not happen to us?" ' Such persons can either be a relation like a mother, father, wife, daughter or someone falling in the category of 'Mahapurusha'. The sacrifice of a close relation is generally out of attachment while the sacrifice of a 'Mahapurusha' is out of compassion. History has produced such great men from time to time. Persons like Gautama Buddha, Dadhichi, Mahatma Gandhi, Subhash Chandra Bose, Bhagat Singh, Guru Gobind Singh, Hazrat Mohammad, Jesus etc., all fall in this category. Their sacrifices were for the whole of humanity and in a way, they were universal friends.

We should not expect sacrifices from our friends to help us in our personal troubles. Therefore, friendship should be restricted to the 'Helpers' and we should be happy if we have some friends falling under this category. The first category is rather worse than an enemy while the second category is no better than acquaintances, and we should accept them that way. Only the third category are true friends and we ourselves should also fall in the same category.

Thus, troubles help us to discover our true friends. Troubles are sent by God for some purpose and this is one of them. With the help of true friends we are not only able to face failures, sorrow, anxiety, or other problems gracefully but it also eases the trouble. The famous poet 'Rahim' has rightly said:

रहिमन विपदा हूँ भली, जो थोरे दिन होय।
हित अनहित या जगत में, जानि परत सब कोय।।

It is good to have trouble for short time. It gives us an opportunity to know who is our well-wisher and who is not.

Why not start to discover a friend right now, instead of waiting for troubles to come first?

A Smile is

a gently curved line .....

..... that can set

a lot of things

straight !

15

A TOTAL VIEW OF LIFE

We see 'life' all around us, yet few of us understand it fully. The perception of 'life' differs from individual to individual depending upon our experiences. To some, life is the greatest blessing and to some, the severest punishment. Others find it somewhere in between. If so, is there any common thread in all these perceptions? This question arose in my mind once and I reflected on it.

It is said that half of life is 'if'. Please note that the middle two letters in the word 'life' are 'i' and 'f'. It is also said that threefourths of life is 'lie'. Note that if 'f' is removed, the remaining word is 'lie'. While this perception of life may be partially true, it does not serve a good purpose if we do not go beyond this. Life has to be seen in totality without missing any letters. The four letters of 'life' should be seen as its four phases and if we follow them faithfully, life becomes enriching and leads us to its ultimate goal. Let us see what these phases are.

The first letter **'L'** indicates the phase of **'Learning'**. This means that the first phase of life is a period of learning. While life continues to be a process of learning all through, it is the initial learning which shapes one's life. During this period, one acquires knowledge of various mundane matters. Right from birth, we have to learn basic activities like sitting, standing, walking and eating as well as educational learning. Good or bad habits acquired during this period influence life in subsequent phases, and this is the time when one is influenced most by the environment in which one grows up. It should be wisely guarded by those who are responsible for the upbringing of children.

Having completed the period of learning, one becomes self-dependent and steps into the second phase of life. This period may be called the period of **'Indulgence'** and the second letter **'I'** stands for it. During this period the society, by and large, gives us independence to lead our life in our own way. It is more so in the present time because individual rights are granted by the constitution and law. One acquires family, wealth, fame, or social standing during this phase of life and enjoys them. One is strong physically and, therefore, there is no anxiety on that account. Depending upon the upbringing, *sanskars* and associates, one also cultivates certain finer qualities but, generally, this is the time for action, for doing things. With the ups and downs of life, one may become more reflective and the process continues as one grows in age and wisdom.

Thus begins the phase of **'Finding'**. This is what the third letter **'F'** indicates. In most cases the period of indulgence is necessary before the urge to find reality arises. In this phase we start understanding the temporariness of mundane matters and events and try to look for something permanent. Slowly, we start giving up the sense of 'doership' and consider ourselves as instruments of God. There may be occasional failures but this awareness is often restored.

Then begins the last phase of life which may be called the period of **'Evolution'**. The last word **'E'** stands for it. Having understood the reality of life, one strives to achieve its ultimate goal and that is the real process of evolution. Every action in this phase of life becomes a step towards the goal and the vicissitudes of life no more bothers one. They only appear as the events of a play on the stage.

When we see life in its totality, it becomes a means to achieve the ultimate goal which is 'evolution' to the level of the 'self'. This may also be called enlightenment, salvation or self-realisation. When life is viewed this way it becomes enriching and every experience becomes a step to evolution. Then even the 'ifs' and 'lies' add to its excitement like the suspense of a stage-drama. Those who fail to look at life in totality get entangled in its 'ifs' and 'lies'. For them 'F' stands for 'Finish' and 'E' for 'End'. Like the drama show on the stage, they keep on repeating the show of life till they reach evolution.

> I expect to pass
> through life but once !
>
> If therefore,
> there be any kindness
> I can show,
> or any good thing
> I can do to any fellow being .....
>
> Let me do it now,
> and not defer or neglect it,
> as I shall not pass
> this way again !
>
> *William Penn*

16
CONSTRUCTIVE DESTRUCTION

In September 1995, as Development Commissioner of Steel I accompanied my boss, the secretary (Steel) on his visit to Gujarat. It was a four-day visit covering a number of places. The visit was a combination of official work and a pilgrimage which made our schedule very hectic, and we had to travel long distances every day, starting early in the morning. This put pressure on our drivers also but fortunately they were very patient. One driver in particular was pious and seemed to have acquired wisdom as a result of his long faithful service.

While travelling from Alang to Somnath, we were discussing several matters in which the driver also participated. During the course of the journey, he gave us a very interesting definition of GOD. The three letters of the word GOD, he said, show the three qualities or *Gunas* of the Almighty, 'G' representing 'Generation', 'O' representing 'Operation' and 'D' representing 'Destruction'. This way they symbolised three in one name, Brahma, Vishnu and Mahesh. The function of Lord Brahma is to generate, Lord Vishnu operates while Lord Mahesh's function is to destroy. If any of these activities is ever stopped, the cycle of life will come to a standstill. Thus, all the three activities are godly and have equal importance. This sounded very interesting as well as logical.

It is easier to accept generation and operation as godly activities but it is not so when we think of destruction. When I reflected on this, it became clear to me that even destruction is a dynamic activity and a necessary link in the chain of life. It also took my mind to Alang, the place we had visited that morning. Alang is a small port in the state of Gujarat which is known for its ship-breaking industry. The special features of the beach make this place suitable for ship-breaking, an activity which has grown at a very fast rate during the past few years and has contributed greatly to the country's economy. The industry is also a major supplier of raw material to certain industries in the steel sector.

The scale of activity at Alang is enormous and one can appreciate this only after visiting the place. While taking us around, the representatives of the industry showed a sense of pride in their contribution to the growth of the steel sector and rightly so.

If we look at the ship-breaking industry from a different viewpoint, it is only a destructive activity. The ships which are built with great effort are cut down to pieces and recycled. How can we call it a developmental or constructive activity? This doubt can be removed if we compare it with the destructive role of God. In this world or universe, whatever has been created has to be destroyed after a certain period. Then only is the flow of life possible. Thus, destruction is an essential part of the lifecycle. While this is true of God's creation, it is equally true of man's creation also. Whatever has been created has to be destroyed one day. And if the phenomenon is a natural one, it becomes a constructive activity. Thus, when a human life comes to an end after it has been lived fully, it is a happy phenomenon. Similarly, if a ship is broken after it has served its purpose, it becomes a developmental or constructive activity. In this way, the ship-breaking industry plays the role of 'Shiv' in the world of steel.

Nature destroys and her destructions are always constructive.

17
SILVER JUBILEE

I graduated in mechanical engineering from the University of Roorkee (now an IIT) in the year 1970. This university celebrates the silver jubilee of all its students twenty-five years after they graduate. Thus our batch's silver jubilee was celebrated in November 1995. I was looking forward to this day with enthusiasm and also made efforts to ensure that many colleagues attended. As a result, as many as one hundred and forty-three colleagues turned up. The celebration went on for the whole day and we had a wonderful time. We recollected our old memories, forgetting our present positions and behaved with each other like we did in our university days.

The University of Roorkee is an old institution with great traditions. Its alumni are generally very close and celebrations like these are held without exception. In addition to the silver jubilee, there is a tradition of celebrating a golden jubilee after fifty years and a diamond jubilee after sixty years of graduation. All these celebrations are held simultaneously. At the time of our silver jubilee, there were twenty-four participants for the golden jubilee and four for the diamond jubilee. It was a pleasure to listen to their accounts of myriad experiences. All of them mentioned the traditions of the university, even though they had faded with time.

I joined the university in 1966 at an early age after passing the first year of my BSc. I had been a good student and had topped in the entrance examination. Till today, this event remains the most pleasant surprise of my life. I came from a semi-rural background with little exposure beyond my class and family. Therefore, joining the University of Roorkee as a topper was something for which I was not exactly prepared. This university had a tradition of giving prominence to the topper, usually called 'senior' and he or she attracted the attention of all. I was no exception and became the victim of extra ragging as a result. Fortunately, the form of ragging in those days was healthy and it helped the new entrants to shed their inhibitions.

I was not very studious and coped with my studies in a relaxed, natural way. I also participated in games and other activities. Fortunately, I maintained my first position through and stood first at the final examinations. I was also declared the best all-rounder of the university and got the Chancellor's gold medal for that achievement. In all, I got nine medals and awards. Subsequently, I joined the IAS and was allotted the U.P. cadre.

I was liked by most of my colleagues and they felt proud of my achievement. I noticed this during the silver jubilee celebration too. Twenty-five years is a long period in one's life and that too, after graduation. This is the period when we have maximum interaction with the world which shapes our personality in the true sense. Close contact with colleagues is possible only rarely and most of us remember only some of their traits. This is true of everyone and one need not be upset if one's personality is not correctly understood by others. This is more so in the case of those who look at life deeply and develop their personalities beyond body and mind. Incidentally, I am one of them and, therefore, try to see a deeper meaning in every interaction. The silver jubilee celebration was no exception and I drew two positive messages from this celebration.

The first is from the fact that even after twenty-five years, my colleagues had great regard for my maintaining the first position throughout my university stay. This fact was proudly mentioned by them whenever I was introduced to anyone. I feel that it is true for all those who maintain their positions, in whatever field they are. Be it in the field of business or any other profession, those who maintain high standards throughout are revered by all, notwithstanding professional rivalries. Of course, the additional requirement is that such positions should be maintained by fair and natural means. Those who keep on shifting their positions are hardly respected. In other words, it is the stability which gives a shining quality to one's personality and this is respected by others.

The second lesson is drawn from the fact that while one hundred and forty-three turned up for the silver jubilee, the number of the golden jubilee participants was twenty-four and those of the diamond jubilee only four. There was no one for the platinum jubilee. I was also told that so far, no one has ever turned up for the platinum jubilee. This fact shows that as one goes on the higher path, the number of companions keeps reducing. The number came down to one-sixth from one jubilee to another and became zero for the platinum jubilee. Therefore, one should not get upset if companions leave gradually as a person continues his journey to a higher path. This should be accepted gracefully.

With this message in mind, my next target is to turn silver into gold.

> The biggest things are always the easiest to do because there is no competition.

18

FALSE CEILING

I served as managing director of the UP Handloom Corporation during the year 1987-88. At that time, this job was considered to be important as well as glamorous. The turnover of the organisation was almost one hundred crores and it had a large number of showrooms all over the country. It was quite a challenging and interesting job to run them efficiently. Every year, a good number of showrooms were renovated and it involved a huge expenditure. One of the expensive items in the renovation was the 'False Ceiling'. This term always amused me and I often wondered why such a beautiful piece of work was called 'False'.

Once I inspected a showroom during its renovation when the work on the false ceiling was in progress. I could, therefore, see the inside of the false ceiling and I found it in bad shape. The wiring, pipe-fittings, ducting, etc., were done badly, probably in the knowledge that they would not be visible after the false ceiling was fitted. The quality of wiring was also poor, which I learnt, was done deliberately in order to increase the frequency of repairs. While I took the necessary steps to correct the situation in the process, I also understood the significance of the word 'false'.

Subsequently, I held many important posts which took me around the country and abroad frequently. I like meeting people and have had an interaction with a large cross-section with widely varying backgrounds. I can modestly claim that I have been able to understand human nature to a great extent and do not get upset easily when someone hurts me or behaves in an unexpected manner. I have found a large number of people who are apparently very well-behaved and project themselves as our well-wishers, while the reality is different. Initially, such a situation used to upset me, but now it is no more so. The incident about the 'false ceiling' also helped me greatly to understand this aspect of human nature. Most people try to hide their faults with false behaviour and a disguised appearance. The reality is known only when we see them closely. Unfortunately, in today's fast world, such opportunities are rare and whenever one tries to do so, the result is a clash or conflict. The only option, therefore, is to watch oneself closely and remove those faults, which we dislike in others.

There is a need to behave well and decently, a desirable quality of a good human being. Good behaviour becomes undesirable only when it is false, but sincerity and genuine goodness will reap rich dividends not only for oneself but for others too. Unfortunately, most of us feel that it is more important to appear nice than to be really nice. It may be true for a short while but it is not so when life is seen in totality. Sooner or later, the false appearance and poor contents inside are exposed and there is no option left but to discard the object in totality. Someone has rightly said, 'It is good to be important but it is more important to be good'. If we believe in this, there would be no need for any 'false ceiling'.

- The shortest and surest way to live with honour in this world is to be in reality what we would appear to be.
- You can cheat some people all the time, all people for sometime but not all the people all the time.

19

PERMANENT OR LESS TEMPORARY

I joined the IAS in 1975. Within twenty years of my service, I changed places twelve times and the number of posts held exceed even this. It had always been difficult to write my permanent address on any document. In the beginning, I gave one or two addresses as permanent but they were always care of someone else. With the change in the quality of relationship with them, the permanence of those addresses also lost its meaning.

Twenty years is a long period in a life and career. Children grow up to adulthood and many family as well as social, responsibilities are added. The volume of personal papers and correspondence in various matters increases greatly. In several matters one has to give a permanent address from time to time. This need arose in my case also and I faced great difficulty in giving such an address, being constrained to give different addresses in different cases, depending upon the convenience at that point of time. It also became difficult for me to remember the address given in a particular matter. All this made me think seriously about settling down at a permanent address.

Fortunately, I had constructed a modest house at Lucknow in the year 1989. It gave me a reasonable rent which augmented my income at a time when expenses were at their peak. Notwithstanding this fact, I decided to settle down in my own house at the earliest, so that there would be no problem relating to a permanent address. Accordingly, I worked on those lines and shifted to my Lucknow house after the completion of my deputation in the Government of India in 1996.

One day, while thinking over the plan to settle down in one place, a philosophical thought came to my mind. The question that arose was: 'Would that really be my permanent address?' The answer, naturally, was in the negative. At best, it would be a less temporary address compared to what I had been writing on forms and documents. After all, there is a limit to the time of stay even at a so-called permanent address. If this is so, how can we call it a permanent address? The world we live in is always changing and all events of life are transitory, so how can one think of a permanent address here? In the final analysis, it becomes only a relative term.

This contemplation opened up my mind. Even though I have shifted to my own house, I have done so taking it not as a permanent address but only as a less temporary one.

Giving and Forgiving

What makes life worth the living
    Is our giving and forgiving.

Giving tiny bits of kindness
    That will leave a joy behind us.

And forgiving bitter trifles
    That the right word often stifles.

For the little things are bigger
    That we often stop to figure.

What makes life worth living
    Is our giving and forgiving.

Thomas Grant Springer

20

MINUS INFINITY TO PLUS INFINITY

Once I was attending a spiritual discourse. The gathering consisted of men as well as women. The subject of the discourse was Lord Krishna and during the course of discussion, the devotion to Lord Krishna was deliberated on. Lord Krishna is loved by most of the women devotees in one form or the other. When Swamiji asked them whether they were devoted to Lord Krishna, almost all of them raised their hands. Then he asked how many of them would like to become the mother of Lord Krishna. Not realising the implications, many showed their willingness. Swamiji then posed the conditions for becoming the mother of Lord Krishna. The first condition was that she and her husband would be imprisoned just after their marriage, by her own brother. The second condition was that Lord Krishna would be the eighth child and the first seven would be killed just after their birth. The third condition was that she would only give birth and the upbringing would be carried out by someone else.

After listening to these conditions, everyone backed out. No one had ever thought so deeply about the price paid by Devaki for giving birth to Lord Krishna. Most of us take such realities as routine matters and hardly think about them deeply unless such events take place in our own lives. The conditions put forward by Swamiji were the facts and the parents of Lord Krishna actually underwent such extreme agony. However, in no account of their sufferings is their bitterness reflected anywhere. This means that the human mind is capable of harmonising harshness even in such painful situations. I have reflected upon this matter deeply and am sharing my thoughts here.

The human mind is capable of a very wide range of reactions to a particular situation as revealed in the way the two characters in the story of Lord Krishna deal with situations confronting them. One is Devaki, mother of Lord Krishna, who could bear the extreme cruelty of her brother without any bitterness. This is the positive dimension of the mind which is achieved through great wisdom. There is no limit to this dimension and it can reach to plus infinity. Questions may be raised about the practicality of this but here we are talking about the possibilities of a positive reaction. Besides Devaki, there are numerous examples of extreme sacrifices made by human beings from time to time in all parts of the world. Most of them made such sacrifices willingly without any bitterness or malice towards anyone. They made such sacrifices for a great cause and derived great satisfaction from their strength drawn from the plus infinity dimension of their minds. Such persons have existed in all times, exist today and shall continue to exist.

Now we look at the second character, Kansa, who was a very powerful but ignorant king. He considered his might and the kingship as permanent. In order to protect his position, he adopted the lowliest possible means, using violence and cruelty to gain his own ends. This is also a dimension of the mind but the negative one. Here also, there is no limit and it can be minus infinity. Such characters too have existed in the past, exist today and will continue to exist in future. They all display the negative dimension of the mind which is the result of ignorance.

Thus the range of the human mind is minus infinity to plus infinity. This also reminds me of integral calculus, a branch of mathematics. Quite often the range of integration is from minus infinity to plus infinity. An integrated mind should be able to accept these ranges objectively and harmonise them. Harmony is possible only by 'knowledge', not mundane but spiritual. Only at a spiritual level harmony can become possible. Life, then, becomes a process of integration of the mind with a range of integration from minus infinity to plus infinity.

21
VARILUX LENS

My eyesight became weak at a very early age. However, no one took notice of it and my hints about not being able to see were not taken seriously. It was only when I went to the Government High School at the district headquarters at twelve years of age, that the vice principal advised me to get my eyes tested. As a result of this delay I had to wear high-powered glasses right from childhood. Subsequently, the power of the glasses increased further and they also became complex.

Like all other technologies, optical technology has advanced greatly in the last thirty years. My first pair of spectacles cost me only nine rupees in the year 1961 while the latest made me poorer by three thousand rupees in 1995. I parted with this amount with great hesitation. My optician had been pleading for it for quite some time, explaining the salient features of the latest glasses known as Varilux Lenses. These lenses are not only light but also have no dividing line between the short-sight and long-sight portions. Their power changes with the distance of the object seen. They are very convenient at an age when one has to wear complex glasses and more so for those whose jobs involve reading and writing. These glasses are not only efficient but also look good.

For some time, I questioned the wisdom behind spending so much for the spectacles. Only after I started feeling comfortable with the glasses and the memory of parting with a huge sum faded, did the questioning come to an end. I also looked at it philosophically and some very interesting lessons came to my mind.

First of all, we should understand the working of an eye. It has a lens and a retina. When an object is seen, its image is formed on the retina which is then noticed by the mind. If for some reason, the image is not formed properly, it is known as an eyesight defect. This defect is corrected with the help of an external lens which is worn in the form of spectacles. Depending upon the nature of the defect, a suitable lens is fitted in them. With the advance in age, the defect becomes complicated and hence more complicated lenses are required. This is where technology has developed. Earlier, two separate spectacles were required for long-sight and short-sight. Subsequently, complex lenses provided both powers in the same lens. Such a lens has a dividing line and requires some practice for adjustment. The latest technology takes care of both these problems. I am not very clear about the exact principle behind the working of a varilux lens but the fact is that its power changes with the distance in a manner which takes care of the movement of the eye. As a result, a correct image is always formed on the retina.

I feel a similar attitude has to be adopted in life also. The world we see around is very complex and if we see it with a fixed focal length, quite often we get aberrated images. Therefore, there is a need to change our attitudes according to the need of the situation so that the mind always receives a good image of the world. Thus, the attitude is like the lens and the mind is like the retina when compared with an eye. If one is able to develop enough wisdom (like optical technology), the change in the attitude with the changing surroundings can become a natural process. In that case, both good and bad can be accepted with equal ease. Living can then become natural and harmonious. The efforts made for such an achievement is worth the outcome.

Having learnt this lesson, I stopped regretting the sum spent on my latest spectacles. Perhaps, the lesson is worth the amount, if not the spectacles.

> - One person says, "Night has fallen," whereas another says, "morning is yet to come".
> - You can lament because roses have thorns or you can rejoice because thorn have roses.

22
COORDINATES OF LIFE

Coordinate geometry is an interesting branch of mathematics. In plane coordinate geometry, there are two axes, namely, 'X' and 'Y', crossing each other at right angles. The point of intersection is known as the origin. The origin is given the coordinates, zero-zero. All other points lying on the plane of these two axes are given coordinates with respect to the origin. Thus, each point has two coordinates known as 'X' and 'Y' coordinates. Depending upon the position of the point, these are either positive or negative or a combination. Since the plane is divided into four quadrants, one quadrant has both the coordinates positive, one both negative and the remaining two quadrants have one coordinate positive and one negative. In graphic form, these may be shown as below:

	Y axis	
Second Quadrant x negative y positive X axis		First Quadrant x positive y positive X axis
	0 origin	
Third Quadrant x negative y negative		Fourth Quadrant x positive y negative
	Y axis	

Based on the relationship of these coordinates, various figures are studied in this branch of mathematics. Starting with a straight line, there are complex figures of various shapes. Overall, the study is very interesting. From two-dimensional geometry we proceed to three-dimensional, which is a little complicated but the basic principles remain the same. Here, the study is made in respect of three-dimensional figures instead of two-dimensional figures.

Viewed philosophically, the basic principles of this branch give some very interesting lessons for life. I intend to share my reflections, confining them to the lessons which can be learnt from two-dimensional coordinate geometry.

Firstly, the four quadrants can be compared with the different states of mind. The quadrant with both positive coordinates indicates the happy state of mind when one feels everything positive in life. The quadrant with both negative coordinates indicates the gloomy state of mind when everything appears to be negative. The remaining two quadrants indicate a mixed state where some aspects appear to be positive and some negative. The lives of most of us pass through these three phases and we accept them as such. In all these phases we dissipate our energy either by enjoying or suffering and eventually depart from the earth. The cycle goes on till we understand the truth and realise it. In fact, the truth lies in rising above both positive and negative. Such a position is possible only at the origin which is the supreme reality, or in other words, God. Till we realise this position, we keep on dissipating our energy, irrespective of our coordinates.

An interesting comparison can also be made with three tendencies, namely *Sattwik*, *Rajasik* and *Tamasik*. The first quadrant represents the *Sattwik* tendencies, the second and fourth represent the *Rajasik* and the third represents the *Tamasik*. Most of us have *Rajasik* tendencies and that is why they occupy two quadrants. Such tendencies motivate us to act for the fulfilment of a desire. If the desire is fulfilled we feel happy and if not, we feel unhappy. On the other hand, the *Sattwik* tendencies always keep us happy while the *Tamasik* keep us unhappy. Again the fact

Coordinates Of Life

is that we stay away from the truth and keep dissipating our energy in all the three situations. The only difference is that in the *Sattwik* situation, energy is used for good purposes, in *Rajasik*, for mixed purposes while in *Tamasik*, for bad purposes. Therefore, the answer lies in rising above all the three tendencies and to become *Gunatita*. This state is possible only when we take our position at the origin which is nothing but the supreme reality or God. This is what is concluded by Lord Krishna also, in the eighteenth chapter of the Gita.

There can be two ways of achieving such a position. One is not to move from the origin, which means that we remain engrossed in God and do not come out in the world at all. This is not possible for most of us who have to lead an active life in the world. The alternative, therefore, is to see God in each happening and object of the world. It means that whatever interaction we have in the world should be seen as emanating from the supreme reality and we should accept it in a detached manner. In that case, everything will appear to be from the origin and the question of positive or negative will not arise at all. In terms of coordinate geometry, it amounts to shifting the axes in such a manner that whatever point we see should appear to be the origin. After all, God is said to be omnipresent and it should not be difficult to see Him everywhere. In coordinate geometry, an exercise for shifting the axes is given occasionally and in life it should be a constant exercise.

> God is a circle whose circumference is nowhere but whose centre is everywhere.

23
TRAFFIC JAM

The number of vehicles is increasing very fast in our country. Over a period of ten years, the total number of vehicles has gone up manifold and the trend continues. While it is a healthy sign of economic development, it is also creating many problems. In India, the road infrastructure has not kept pace with the increase in the traffic, resulting in the crowding of roads, particularly in big cities. Earlier, Calcutta was known for its traffic jams but now other metropolitan cities have become worse. In addition, the problem of pollution is also reaching unmanageable proportions. While legislative measures are being taken to tackle pollution, their poor implementation makes the situation worsen day by day.

For few years I had the opportunity of living in Delhi and Calcutta. Quite often I also faced the problem of traffic jams. At times I was able to change my route or would not venture out, just to avoid traffic jams but normally they had to be faced. Once we get stuck in a traffic jam, it becomes very difficult to come out as a number of vehicles surround us and we have to follow the race. In such moments, I generally took a very amused view of the situation and compared it with the growing rat race in the society. This contemplation has taught me some valuable lessons.

In today's materialistic world, the number of desires entertained is considered to be an important criterion of progress, and for most of us, it is the sole criterion. The increasing emphasis on consumerism is an indication of the acquisitiveness of today. Even the TV programmes are full of commercial advertisements and create the unnecessary desire to acquire more and more things. I compare this increase in the number of desires with the increasing number of vehicles on the roads. Like the number of vehicles, human desires have also increased manifold in recent times, resulting in a materialistic rat race.

While the increase in the number of desires up to a certain extent and their fulfilment is a healthy sign, beyond a point they choke us materially, mentally as well as physically. It is more so when resources do not permit such an increase. This is like the road infrastructure in relation to the vehicle population. Unless the roads are widened accordingly or new roads are constructed, the increasing number of vehicles is bound to choke them. Similarly, unless our income increases proportionately or new sources of income are created, it is not possible to fulfil the increasing number of desires and they are bound to choke our resources.

Comfortable living and the use of modern appliances can be quite helpful if one is able to afford them and also maintain a healthy mental attitude towards them. Such an attitude will not create the pollution of negative thoughts. Unfortunately, this is not happening. The more we progress materially, the more we are becoming envious and jealous of each other. In the process, we are not always able to enjoy the fruits of our own progress, nor of others. Our negative thoughts keep polluting the environment and the pleasure of our acquisitions is also lost. We either take no steps to stop this mental pollution or do not act upon them. The situation is like taking legislative measures to control vehicle pollution without implementing them properly. Not many of us read good books or live in the company of wise people, who, in any case, have few followers.

It is also not possible to fulfil the increasing number of desires of all the people. In fact there are not enough resources to meet them. Unnecessary desires can be fulfilled only by a small percentage of people, thus creating disharmony. Generally, such desires cannot be met by honest means. The kind of corruption we see all around today is mainly due to unnecessary desires of the people. Even if one is able to fulfil such desires, in the final analysis, one finds them not worthwhile. By the time one realises so, it is too late and one has to endure the consequent agony, much like the situation of a person trapped in a traffic jam. He can neither move further nor change his path. All progress at that time comes to a halt.

What is the way out? The way out is to choose the correct goal, the correct path and the correct means of transport. A good number of vehicles on the road are moving without any goal, going from place to place due to restlessness. After choosing the correct goal, choose the right path. At times, the goal is achieved quicker by taking a longer route which may be less crowded and it is not always necessary to be in the rat race. Also, do not change lanes every now and then, most traffic jams being due to such changes. The correct means of transport is also important. At times one can reach the destination quicker on foot than in a luxurious car. After all, the vehicle is just a means and not the end. Lastly, choose the correct timings. It is better to start early. Taking care of these factors, a traffic jam can be avoided to a great extent, be it on the road or in life. In that case even occasional jams can be enjoyed as they give us an opportunity to watch our own position closely.

> The trouble with the rat race is that even if you win, you are still a rat.

24
OHM'S LAW OF LIFE

In my IAS entrance examination I opted for two papers of physics. Though I had not been a student of physics, the study of the subject during my engineering course had given me enough confidence. I remember that my score in one paper of physics was the highest among those who were selected. I also remember one exercise in that paper on Ohm's Law. It was a simple numerical question of forty marks whose solution required only a few lines.

Most of the candidates were puzzled to see such a simple question carrying forty marks and I was no exception. However, the question was tricky and required a clear conception of Ohm's law. Fortunately, I could understand the trick and solved it as the first question feeling quite happy about scoring forty marks in the first ten minutes. When the candidates came out of the examination hall, that question was the topic of discussion. Each one was giving his own interpretation and the answers varied widely from candidate to candidate. This created a very interesting scene as our selection depended on this question. Fortunately, my answer was correct and that was largely responsible for my selection as well as the highest score in the paper.

I have narrated this incident many times. The interesting fact was that most of those who had obtained a master's degree or even a doctorate in physics had committed a mistake in solving the question. They could not believe that a question of forty marks could be that simple. As a result they had interpreted the question in their own way and gone off the track. Perhaps, they did not have a clear understanding of the Ohm's law and made a mistake. Subsequently, I contemplated over the incident and related it to one simple aspect of life.

The fundamental laws of living are so simple that we often fail to understand them and make our lives complicated. If we draw a simile from Ohm's law, the electric current may be compared with the motivation to live and the objective is to have a continuous flow of motivation in good quantity. For this, there has to be a source of power. Such a source can either be a battery or power line. When the source is a battery, the current flows for a limited period depending upon the strength of the battery and the resistance in the circuit. If we wish the current to flow for all time, the battery should either be replaced or recharged. In case the source is a power line, such replacement or recharging is not required. The energy in that case will come directly from the power house and as long as the power station works, the current will continue to flow.

The second factor on which the amount of current depends is the resistance. The lower the resistance, the higher is the amount of current. In case the resistance becomes zero, the current will become infinite and the conductor in such a case becomes a superconductor. Super conductivity is the latest development in science, and it is said that it can solve the energy problem to a great extent because there is no loss of energy in a superconductor.

In life, the source of motivation can either be material objects or divine power. Material objects like name, fame, wealth, position, etc., give us a strong motivation to live but all these sources are transitory, like a battery. After a time they stop giving motivation and need either replacement or recharging. On the other hand, if divinity is the source of motivation like a powerhouse, there is no question of its depletion. The motivation to live then continues till we ourselves become part of divinity.

The equivalent of resistance in life is our ego. The more dominant the ego, the more is the loss of our energy. Therefore, the aim should be to reduce our ego as much as possible. If we become totally egoless, the current will become infinite and, perhaps, that is the stage of reaching divinity itself. However, as long as we live in the world, it may not be possible.

Therefore, the conclusion is that if we connect ourselves with the divine power house with full sense of surrender, we shall experience infinite life current flowing through us like a superconductor and there will be no loss of energy. This is what is called Ohm's law in physics and we may call it *Om's Law in Life*.

Choose your Words !

A careless word may kindle strife,
A cruel word may wreck a life.

> A bitter word may hate instil,
> A brutal word may even kill.

A gracious word may smooth the way,
A joyous word may make some life gay.

> A timely word may lessen stress,
> A loving word may heal and bless.

25

THE DIVINE COURT

There are three main pillars of democracy, namely, the legislature, the executive and the judiciary. As the press also plays an important role in democracy, it may be called the fourth pillar. If all the four pillars are strong and play their role properly, we can create an ideal society to live in. They also keep a check on each other, and this is a very important aspect of our Constitution which has, by and large, worked well.

This check and balance system is very obviously reflected in recent times when the courts have exercised their powers in the larger interest of the society. People in general have welcomed this development because they feel that the other three pillars of the democracy have not played their roles properly. From this point of view, the judiciary has done a great service to the system. However, the real solution lies in each organ playing its role properly and we hope that they will.

In the judicial system, there is a hierarchy starting from the lowest court to the Supreme Court. Of course, the judicial process in general is so slow that justice is often delayed. In many cases it amounts to justice denied. Even if it is not denied, we cannot say for sure that justice is always done by the courts. After all, there is a process of law which is full of lacunas and chances of committing errors are quite high, despite all the good intentions and best efforts on the part of those who are involved in the dispensation of justice. Such errors may be committed at the level of the apex court also but there is no forum to approach thereafter, as far as the mundane world is concerned.

Is this really so ? I had a chance to contemplate over this subject many years back when I was posted as a district magistrate. One day, a smart young boy came to see me in my office. He was an officer of the Indian Forest Service and came to me in connection with the parole of his father who was in jail, undergoing a life sentence. I had rejected the case on the previous day only in a routine manner because it was not recommended by the relevant officers. The young boy told me that he was going to be married soon and the parole of his father was required for that purpose. He had brought an invitation card of the marriage for my perusal. He also told me that his father was a school teacher and had been implicated falsely in a murder case. They had fought the case up to the High Court but beyond that they could not afford more litigation. I felt sympathetic towards the boy on account of his manners and the purpose for which the parole was sought. Though the case had been rejected, I recalled the file and recorded the new facts brought to my notice. I made a recommendation for release, overruling my previous recommendation and eventually the parole was granted.

Perhaps, the boy and his father felt personally grateful to me. After the marriage was over and the time for going back to jail had come, both of them came to see me to express their gratitude. The father had also brought two books written by him. I do not remember their exact subject but they were a reflection of his inner growth. All this touched me greatly and I felt like hearing the story behind his conviction, which he narrated briefly. On hearing this story, my inner conscience felt that he was really innocent. So I asked him a very personal question, notwithstanding my official position. The question was how he felt about his conviction for life without being guilty, if he was innocent. He gave a very enriching reply which I am sharing here.

He said that in the beginning, he had felt very anguished and had questioned the validity of not only the man-made laws but also the divine laws. However, by the grace of God, he soon became contemplative and started accepting reality. Gradually the acceptance turned into faith. He then felt that all events in life happen under cause and effect laws, which can be called divine laws, and man-made laws were just part of them. While there may be errors in the dispensation of justice through the man-made system, there is no chance of such an error in the dispensation of divine justice. In his case, perhaps, the same thing had happened and his conviction must have been the result of divine justice. Once viewed that way, he was trying to make the best use of the situation for his inner growth.

Very few of us can accept the harsh realities of life so gracefully. However, once the fundamentals of divine laws are understood, the acceptance becomes natural. Then one starts seeing the grace of God even in the seemingly bad events of life. Perhaps, the errors committed by mundane courts is one way of dispensing justice by the Divine court.

Stop one Heart breaking !

If I can stop one heart from breaking,
I shall not live in vain.

> If I can ease one life the aching,
> Or cool one pain ;
> Or help one lonely person
> Into happiness again.

I shall not live in vain.

Emily Disckinson

26

GOD AS AN ACCOUNTANT

On August 15,1995, I was invited by Fort Williams' Central School, Calcutta, as the chief guest. The invitation was extended by the principal more as a personal equation than official. After the hoisting, I was asked to garland a picture of Sri Aurobindo. At that time I learnt that August 15th was his birthday. I did not know it earlier though I always had deep reverence for him. The principal of the school was a devotee of Sri Aurobindo and, perhaps, that was the reason for such a ceremony.

Before this, I had tried to read one or two books of Sri Aurobindo but found them difficult to understand despite my interest in spiritual literature. This event, however, created in me a desire to know more about him. So soon after, I bought a biography of Sri Aurobindo and read it. Many aspects of his life influenced me deeply and I am going to share here one which affected me most.

Sri Aurobindo was born on August 15,1872 at Calcutta. His father, Krishna Dhan Ghosh, was a completely anglicised person, as he had studied for an M D in England. He was posted as a civil surgeon with the British government. Sri Aurobindo grew up in an anglicised atmosphere at home. When he was five years old, he was sent, along with his two elder brothers, to the Loretto Convent School at Darjeeling, run by an Irish nun. There the three brothers had only European boys as friends and companions, for it was a school meant only for English children. Later, they were sent to England and thus Sri Aurobindo grew up in entire ignorance of India, her people, her religion and her culture.

During the course of his stay in England, he mastered French and learnt enough of Italian and German.

His father wanted him to join the ICS but destiny had something altogether different in store for him. In deference to his father's wish, he passed the ICS examination with distinction but his heart was not in the service, which he had joined only to comply with his father's wish. He neglected his lessons in riding and purposely failed so that he could escape from the bondage of the ICS. By this time he had started taking an interest in Indian politics and was looking for an opportunity to return to India. At this point of time he came in contact with the ruler of the state of Baroda, who appointed him in his service at a salary of Rs. 200 a month. He left England in January 1893 and joined the state service of Baroda.

Sri Aurobindo was very simple in his mode of living. He did not care much for food or dress, because he never attached any importance to them. He never visited the market for his clothes. At home, he dressed in a plain white *chaddar* and *dhoti*, and outside invariably in white drill suits. He had no love of money. He used to get a lumpsum of three month's pay in a bag which he emptied in a tray lying on his table. He never bothered to keep money in a safe under lock and key. He did not keep an account of what he spent.

One day a close friend asked him why he was so careless about his money. He laughed and then replied, "Well, it is proof that we are living in the midst of honest and good people". "But you never keep an account which may testify to the honesty of the people around you?" the friend asked him. Then with a serene face Sri Aurobindo replied, "It is God who keeps account for me. He gives me as much as I want and keeps the rest to Himself. At any rate, He does not keep me in want, then why should I worry?" This is what influenced me most. Most of us waste our life in keeping accounts. Sri Aurobindo had a great mission in life and, therefore, he considered this activity to be too trivial. He left it to God and was confident that He would keep the accounts in good shape and at the same time would not keep him in want. And it is true that money is never a problem for a truly selfless mission. For such a mission, money comes from unexpected sources. The same is true with a selfless life. God takes care of the needs of such a person and works as an accountant for him. The secret, however, is that He takes care of only the needs and not the greed.

> *Money may buy the Husk of things....*
>
> *but not the Kernel !*
>
> *It may buy Food.... but not Appetite !*
>
> *Medicine... but not Health !*
>
> *Bed.... but not Sleep !*
>
> *Acquaintances.... but not Friends !*
>
> *Servants.... but not Faithfulness !*
>
> *Pleasure.... but not Peace or Happiness !*

27

WHEN YOU KEEP YOUR WORD

I often recall a small event of 1983 when I was posted as collector of a district, where in an old Sanskrit college, a function was being organised. The management of the institution had approached me before the function to be the chief guest. The institution was located at a distance from the district headquarters and I was not sure of being able to spare sufficient time for the programme which meant a long journey too. Moreover, I did not consider myself to be the appropriate chief guest for such an institution. However, on insistence from the management, I had agreed.

Soon the day of the function arrived. It was in the afternoon and I had some very important papers to see at the headquarters. I was in a dilemma about whether to go for the programme or not, knowing that a collector can always excuse himself on some pretext or the other. That temptation came to my mind also. But in the meanwhile, one member of the management had come to my office to accompany me to the institution, so I reluctantly went with him. In my mind I was not sure whether the time spent on the function would be worthwhile or not.

At that time I had become a life member of the Bharatiya Vidya Bhavan and its fortnightly journal used to reach me regularly. Usually, I read it while travelling, and on that day since the latest issue was with me, I went through the Bhavan's journal. Apart from the text, this journal contains some sayings and thoughts from various sources written prominently in spare spaces. These thoughts are normally very inspiring. That day, soon after we started, I came across a thought which was like this: "Fortunate are those who keep their promise, be it good or sinful". This single sentence removed all my hesitation and I became enthusiastic about the programme which was organised very well. We all felt very happy about it.

This incident made me contemplate. All of us face situations when we find it difficult to keep our word or promise. Those who are sensitive face a conflict in the mind, particularly when sufficient reasons do not exist for not keeping one's word or promise. Quite often even such persons give untrue reasons for not keeping them, doing this mainly to satisfy themselves rather than others. Gradually, this becomes a habit; no wonder today we find many responsible persons whose word or promises have no meaning and who keep others in uncertainty even without sufficient justification.

My contemplation in this regard has led me to the conclusion that for a sincere and truthful person, situations of such conflict hardly arise. Once we are firm in our resolve that we shall always keep our word or promise, events occur in such a manner that they are kept effortlessly. After the above-mentioned incident, I made it almost a *sadhana* to keep my word unless a situation arose when not keeping them became my duty. In that case, there has been no feeling of guilt or uneasiness. Gradually, a stage comes when we speak only those words which we are able to abide by effortlessly. Nature also creates circumstances accordingly. Personally, I have experienced many situations where I was surprised by the turn of events which made it possible to honour a commitment. The same situation then extends to our thoughts and we entertain only those thoughts which are actually converted into action. I am not giving any specific events here because the intention is only to make a point.

Here it is clarified that the point made is not as simple as it appears. The whole process requires a great deal of wisdom and maturity. To reach a stage when one's words or thoughts are taken care of by nature, one has to undergo constant refinement and ripening. The first step is that words should be spoken after a great deal of thinking, and casual speaking should come to a stop. "Think before you speak and not vice versa" has to be always kept in mind. It is better to keep silent if we are not sure of ourselves. One can always choose suitable words to deal with a particular situation in order to avoid further embarrassment. Once we start doing so, our words have a weight of meaning and others take us seriously. The process starts from here.

The second important step is that a promise or thought of action should arise as a result of duty, keeping in view the means available to us at a particular point of time. At times duty demands certain action on our part but means may not permit it. In such a situation, promises should be given accordingly. Thirdly, while giving promises one should be free from anger, envy, hatred or sentiments. Words spoken in such a state of mind normally create a difficult situation and disturb one's peace of mind in the long run. Lastly, we must mean what we say and apply ourselves fully to keep our word. Nature helps us primarily through ourselves, and when we apply ourselves sincerely, conditions are so created that others also help.

Once the above requirements are met, the process becomes natural and we are effortlessly able to keep our word. In fact, our will in that case becomes His will and we consider ourselves only the instruments. Even an apparently sinful act then becomes a part of our *sadhana* and leads to perfection.

> Refusing in a kind manner is better than making promises which are not kept.

28
GANDHIJI'S MONKEY

I was posted as the managing director of the UP Spinning Company at Kanpur in September 1989. Soon after I took charge, I had a very interesting visitor from an eastern district of UP — Ghazipur. He was completely blind and reached my office with great difficulty. He was a stranger to me and, therefore, I received him with some surprise. I could not guess what the purpose of his visit was. After he settled down on a chair, I politely asked him what he wanted. He said he had no purpose except to meet me. He had heard of me when I was the collector of his neighbouring district about five years back and had developed a wish to see me. He was very happy to have fulfilled his wish that day, though it had been quite difficult for him to travel from Ghazipur and then to reach my office.

Accepting what he said, I switched on to a general discussion and asked about the cause of his blindness. He told me that he had lost his eyesight in his early childhood during an attack of smallpox. The way he narrated his story gave an indication that he had accepted the reality gracefully and had no bitterness in his mind. This encouraged me to ask a few more personal questions. When I asked whether he missed seeing the world around, he gave a very philosophical reply, saying that there was not much to see in this transitory world which was full of evil. By not being able to see, he was saved from this evil. As a result he always contemplated on God, to see Whom no physical eyes were required. I was touched by his answer and respected his philosophy. After sometime, he left my office and we never met again.

This visitor left a great mark on my mind and I usually reflect on what he said. This also reminds me of Gandhiji's three monkeys, one of whom keeps his eyes shut, the other his ears closed and the third his mouth. The significance of this is that one should avoid seeing evil, listening to evil and speaking evil. This is a necessary condition for inner growth which is the main objective of life. After all, a child is born with a pure mind but as he grows and has interaction with the outer world, his mind entertains evil thoughts which ultimately cause disharmony in society in addition to his own downfall. If, therefore, by some act of God or by controlling the mind, the influence of evil can be kept away, inner growth is accelerated. By this, the inference should not be drawn that in order to grow internally, one has to be physically blind, deaf or dumb. This state is only symbolic. The ultimate requirement is to remain uninfluenced by evil either physically or mentally.

The gentleman who met me had seen his disability in this light and made use of it for his inner growth. He was almost an illiterate person but had grown into a wise person by constant contemplation. To me he appeared to be a monkey of Gandhiji who kept his eyes closed in order to avert them from evil.

Laughter is the jam on the toast of life.

It adds flavour,

keeps it from being too dry,

and makes it easier to swallow !

Diane Johnson

29

INSPIRATION FROM THE VOID

My two-year posting at Calcutta from July 1994 to July 1996 gave me a very good opportunity to go to various places in Bengal and also to meet a large cross-section of people with different backgrounds. Calcutta itself is a culturally rich city where material considerations are lesser than similar other cities in the country. It boasts of very good institutions here and one is likely to come across many great personalities as well as a wealth of information. I could not scan much of the city because of the nature of my job but despite that, I met many wise and learned persons and learnt valuable things from them. One such person was Pratap Chander Chunder who had been the Union Education Minister in the Janata Government of 1977, and was currently the chairman of Bhartiya Vidya Bhawan, Calcutta centre.

Once I visited P C Chunder with the Kendra Director, K V Gopalakrishnan. He lived in the old part of the city in his ancestral house. The family had been in the legal profession for generations and Shri Chunder himself was a practising lawyer at the Calcutta High Court. When we met him, he was sitting in his office. I found that his office furniture was very old and he himself appeared so simple that I was surprised. We talked on various subjects for about half an hour. During our discussion, some reference was made to the attitude towards life and I said that life was like a glass of water which is half full and half void and we should look at the filled portion of it. To this he gave a very interesting response by saying that the void portion is equally important as one can get a lot of inspiration from it. I could understand the point immediately and we did not discuss it further. Subsequently, I contemplated over this piece of advice and tried to analyse it further.

It is true that in this imperfect world, no life can be full in the true sense. However, making it full is the main objective of life and the imperfections of the world have to be seen as opportunities to do so. Seen from this viewpoint the void of life becomes very important because they set goals for us and make us strive to achieve them. While one should make the best use of what is already achieved, one has to work earnestly for what has yet to be achieved. The determination to do so comes only from the void portion. If one keeps looking at the filled portion only, such inspiration and determination may not come at all. Here we are not talking of the materialistic rat race of common parlance. The reference is to those achievements which help in taking us to the goal of life. Of course, needful material achievements also fall in this category.

If we look at the voids of life this way, they can give us a lot of inspiration and gradually it should be possible to lead a totally fulfilled life. Such a life is a really enriched one and will help us reach the goal of life. The voids in the lives of others should also be seen in the same way and they should be inspired to fill them. Thus, we can help each other in making life richer and reduce the imperfection or the voids of the world.

> Be what you are. This is the first step towards becoming better than you are.

30
THE FALL OF SHIVALIK

After I joined at Calcutta in July 1994, I wanted to join a club for tennis. Calcutta is known for its clubs and there are many which provide good facilities for the game, the South Club of Calcutta being considered the best, as it has produced many national level players. I used to watch tennis in this club from the balcony of my friend's house during my visits to Calcutta prior to my posting and always entertained a desire to play there. This wish of mine was fulfilled when a friend arranged for me to play there soon after I shifted to Calcutta. That friend himself, though bulky, was a good player of tennis and we soon developed a liking for each other.

My friend used to live in a five-storey building called 'Shivalik' which was located in central Calcutta. His flat was on the fifth floor. Being somewhat bulky, he usually complained about it as the occasional climb up was arduous. I always advised him to look at the positive features of the flat and to accept gladly what providence had provided him. From the viewpoint of location and layout, it was a good flat and, therefore, he had all reason to feel happy. He, however, never took my word as seriously as I wished him to. The matter ended there.

After about a year, one morning, the newspapers of Calcutta carried the headlines about the sudden sinking of the 'Shivalik' building into the ground. The news did not give a clear picture about the inmates and only mentioned that efforts were being made to rescue them. This created great anxiety and we tried to enquire about our friend. After sometime we learnt that he had been successfully rescued along with his wife and daughter. His only son also survived as he had left for IIT, Chennai, only a few days back. This gave us tremendous relief though it was eclipsed by the fact that all the inmates of the other flats died and it turned out to be a great tragedy in the city. The newspapers carried the news related to this mishap for many days. In due course, the builder was also arrested.

When I met my friend after the mishap, he had not fully recovered from the shock, but showed great respect towards the advice I used to give him about the flat. It was only because his flat was on the top floor, that he had survived the mishap. That was the only floor which remained above the ground, while the other four sank completely. Subsequent enquiries revealed that the foundation of the building had not been prepared properly which was why the soil had given way. Due to commercial reasons, undue haste was also shown in the construction of the building. The Calcutta Municipal Corporation became more alert when sanctioning building plans after this accident.

I thought over this event from two points of view. One was the providential escape of my friend which changed his attitude greatly. The second was about the role of the foundation in the construction of a building. If the foundation is not prepared properly, there is always a danger of its falling. The same is true for nation-building. When I see the falling values in our nation, I always feel that, perhaps, something has gone drastically wrong in its very foundation. Therefore, there is a need to take corrective measures, otherwise the day may not be far away when its collapse will come like the fall of the 'Shivalik' building of Calcutta. No purpose will then be served by complaining about the weak foundation. We must, therefore, learn appropriate lessons without any delay and start taking corrective steps. No beginning is too late. Our nation is great and has survived many a crisis in its long history because of its strong foundation. Now that the entire nation-building is on a weak foundation, the collapse is a very distinct possibility.

The same logic is applicable in the case of individuals, families and societies. If the very foundation of development is faulty, how can we think of a healthy development? In all these cases, it is the character which acts as the foundation. If we want strong and durable nation-building, there is no option but to have a strong foundation for the national character.

> When one door
>
> of happiness closes
>
> another opens .....
>
> But often, we look so long
>
> and so regretfully
>
> upon the closed door .....
>
> That we do not see
>
> the new door
>
> which has been opened for us !
>
> *Helen Keller*

31

DIALLING CODE OF GOD

The Brahma Kumaris Ishwariya Vishwa Vidyalaya organised a four-day All India Conference for administrators, executives and managers from 12 to 15 October, 1996, at its international headquarters at Mount Abu in Rajasthan. This organisation had set up an 'Academy for a Better World' and called its campus 'Gyan Sarovar'. It was a new complex located at Mount Abu and was the venue of the conference. The participants, exceeding six hundred in number, came from all over the country and from all kinds of organisations, government as well as non-government. The theme of the conference was "Value-Based Administration — Prospects and Challenges". All the participants highly appreciated the contents as well as the arrangements for the conference. This complex easily compared with any modern international venue while maintaining its serene and spiritual environment. The organisation of the conference was a part of the diamond jubilee celebration of the Brahma Kumaris Organisation. I had the honour to attend the conference as a guest speaker.

The Brahma Kumaris Organisation came up in the year 1937 and has since spread all over the world on account of its dedicated and useful services rendered in all fields. The main aim of the organisation is to make this world a better place to live in by making each human being a better person. The approach is to make each individual realise his true potential as everyone is a child of God. Most of us forget this reality in the rush and clamour of the world and confine ourselves to our bodies only, while the true potential is in our 'Atma'. The body is mortal while the 'Atma' is immortal and is a part of 'Paramatma' which is 'God' or 'Supreme Reality'. This way we all are children of God and if we can establish this relationship, we develop Godly qualities and become better persons for society. Not only this, we enjoy tremendous peace of mind and all good qualities come to us effortlessly. Thus, we achieve true happiness which is never disturbed by the vicissitudes of the world.

While there were sessions on different aspects of administration and management addressed by eminent speakers from different fields, the day would begin with Raja Yoga classes. 'Raja Yoga' is a way of connecting ourselves with God and in the process becoming our own king, living like a 'Raja' irrespective of our external conditions. However, it is not as simple as it appears. For this, one has to make a very determined and sustained effort but it is worth the results. After all, even for transitory success in this worldly life, we face and tackle so many troubles while here we get something which is eternal. I feel that the 'Raja Yoga' classes were the best part of the conference. The speaker who explained the principle of 'Raja Yoga' was a very senior member of the Brahma Kumaris Organisation. Her deliberation was extremely logical and interesting. While I have no intention of going into the details nor am I capable of doing so, I am touching upon an interesting part of the talk on 'Raja Yoga'.

For making contact with the Kingdom of God, we have to call Him up. To do so we must know His dial code but most of us do not know it. In 'Raja Yoga' classes, this code was disclosed as '0001' and it was beautifully explained. In our worldly connections also we now have STD codes. For reaching any part of our country the code begins with '0' and if we want to reach the Kingdom that is New Delhi then '0' is to be followed by '1'. Similarly, for international dialling, the code begins with '00' and if we want to reach the Kingdom of the world which we can safely consider to be USA, then '00' is again to be followed by '1'. In order to reach the Kingdom of God, one has to rise even above the world and therefore one more '0' is required followed by '1'. Thus, by dialling '0001' we reach the kingdom of God and we may call it the dialling code of God.

While it is interesting when seen in a light vein, there is great depth in its connotations and very few are fortunate enough to reach the Kingdom, though everyone of us is capable of doing so. For this, one has to understand the meaning of the zeros of the code. The zeros mean that in order to rise above the world, we have to reduce ourselves to zeros at various levels. It is like the launching of a rocket in which the ascent begins only after we count down up to zero. While in our worldly ascent, one zero is enough, we require three zeros for Godly ascent. The first zero implies that we have to give up material pleasures and have to develop detachment from them. It does not necessarily mean that we have to give them up physically. It only means that mentally they should have 'zero' meaning for us, if we wish to reach God. The second 'zero' implies that we have to rise above persons also. However pleasant a human relationship may be, it is only a body relationship and hence transitory. It is, therefore, essential to rise above all body relations, which means that we must reduce our human relations to zero. Again, it does not mean giving them up physically but mentally one has to be above them.

Having transcended material and body relations, one has to rise above the mind. It means that we must rise above our thoughts also. The thoughts arise in the mind which is a part of the body. Therefore, in order to reach the Kingdom of God, we have to transcend our own bodily senses completely. This is what is implied by the third 'zero'. Having done so, we become one with God and that is what is meant by the digit '1'.

Thus the dial code of God very well explains the way to reach Him. It is a hard process and requires a great deal of determination on our part but the outcome is more than worth the efforts. According to me, this was the conclusion of the conference. The closer we reach God, the easier it is for us to imbibe the values and value-based administration becomes a natural outcome in all fields of life.

> Realisation one takes beyond virtue and vice, beyond future and past; beyond all pains of opposites.

32
FROM KNOWN TO UNKNOWN

I was posted at Gorakhpur in August 1980 as Regional Food Controller. This posting in itself was a turning point in my life. Before this I was at Meerut and was transferred to Lucknow in March 1980. The events turned in such a way that I had to seek a change only after a few months and went to Gorakhpur.

My post at Gorakhpur was a regional one under the divisional commissioner. My Commissioner was a pious person and I worked with him for three years, in the final year as Collector in the same division. His personality left a deep mark on my life. Our families too came close together and developed a mutual liking. He had three daughters and one son, Amitabh, who was the youngest. The boy was bright and influenced all those who came in close contact with him by his manners, intelligence and courage. I, in particular, developed a great fondness for him which grew with time.

The boy did not enjoy good health right from his childhood. His body suffered from a lack of resistance, and soon it was found to be a kidney defect. At that time he had hardly entered his teens. He was operated upon for a kidney transplant which was donated by his mother. All through he displayed tremendous courage and continued his studies without much disturbance, thus giving hopes to all those who came in touch with him. Unfortunately, after a few years, the problem appeared again and he had to undergo another kidney transplantation. This time the donor was his sister. The operation was successful, and soon Amitabh was full of courage and hope. He completed his graduation and joined the Indian Institute of Foreign Trade (IIFT) at New Delhi for his MBA course.

I had been in contact with Amitabh all through but the closer contact came in Delhi when he came to join IIFT. I was his local guardian and he used to stay with us frequently. My whole family had a liking for him and our affection grew as we came closer. I was deeply influenced by his courage and nicknamed him 'Fighter'. At times we used to get depressed but he never displayed any sign of sadness or self-pity. Despite all his problems he never expected any help from others. Instead, he was a source of inspiration for them. I always felt the depth in him but not to its fullest extent. Occasionally, we used to discuss the philosophy of life but, perhaps, the generation gap was a barrier in reaching to his depths.

Soon after the completion of his MBA, Amitabh joined MMTC at Delhi and I was transferred to Calcutta. Our contact thus reduced to a great extent, though I continued to enquire about him. His body resistance had came down once again and it became difficult for him to continue at Delhi. As a result he had to shift to his parent's home at Lucknow for a new job. However, things were gradually becoming difficult.

I returned to Lucknow in July 1996 after my deputation and once again came close to Amitabh. By this time his condition had become serious. He had to discontinue his job and was confined to bed. I visited him several times and he used to feel very happy when I did. At times we said nothing, though we communicated a lot. Talking of courage and hope had lost its meaning as the outcome was known to him and to those around. Now it was only a question of facing the reality with courage and hope. He left for his unknown destination on 3 January, 1997, destined not to enjoy the new year.

Amitabh had grown very contemplative during his last years. Perhaps, he was always so but gave more expression to his thoughts towards the end of his journey. He used to do it silently and rarely shared his thoughts with anybody. Perhaps, he expected others to measure his depth and did not want to disclose it while he was alive. He left ample proof of his depth in the form of many jottings which are like pebbles on the vast seashore of life. One has to find, collect and understand them. They are the true measures of his depth. One such jotting goes like this:

> There are things Known,
> And things Unknown,
> And in between are the doors.

Amitabh has conveyed the whole philosophy of life in these few words. The journey of life is always from known to unknown. Whether it is a mundane or spiritual matter, our goal is to know the unknown. It is only a question of finding the door, which definitely exists but someone has to show it to us. Amitabh has done the same by his physical extinction. He is like a "Guru" described by Kabir in his 'doha':

> गुरु गोबिन्द दोनों खड़े, काकू लागे पॉय।
> बलिहारी गुरु आपनो, गोबिंद दियो बताय।।

His father paid him a fitting tribute when he said: 'Till his death he was my son and now I consider him to be my Guru'. Who says Amitabh died? Amitabh never dies. It only sets to rise again.

The father and mother give birth to body; the Guru gives birth to soul.

33

ROOM FOR IMPROVEMENT

I started writing about my experiences of life and lessons learnt from them from the year 1990. In that year the 'Kabir Peace Mission' had been founded. The purpose of creating such a mission was to develop positive thinking in the society. The mission also decided to bring out a small quarterly journal in the name of Kabir Jyoti. Basically, it was a compilation work with contents taken from various sources. However, I used to contribute an article in each issue based on my experiences in life. The objective was to draw a positive message from every experience. In due course, I developed a fondness for writing and inspiration came quite naturally. In 1991, I went to Delhi on central deputation and since then the process accelerated. By the end of 1994, I had a good collection of my writings.

My friends and well-wishers spoke well about the style and the message of my articles. What they liked most was that the message was based on real-life experience and it was narrated in a short and simple manner. They also advised me to get them printed in the form of a book. This encouraged me to think along those lines. By this time I had developed a good communication with my publisher and my first book *Dictionary of Positive Thoughts* had already been published by him. However, there was a difference between the two books. The first one was a compilation of thoughts taken from various sources and there was hardly anything personal about them except the selection. The latter book, on the other hand, was totally personal views meant to inspire others. Since one could never be sure of their impression on the readers, I decided to further test their effect on various readers. To do so I prepared a few sets and circulated them among those whom I considered balanced and mature enough for a reliable feedback.

Almost all those who went through the articles gave me a positive feedback and therefore, I decided to go in for their publication in the form of a book. When approached, the publisher immediately agreed to do so. I had also given a set to my spiritual master for his blessings and guidance. While approving the idea of publication, he advised me to pay greater attention towards the editing of the book and I took his advice seriously. Then I was to decide about the 'Foreword' for the book. For this, I requested my director at that time of the National Academy of Administration, for whom I had a high regard and who also knew me well. He gladly agreed and wrote a very inspiring 'foreword'. He was generally appreciative of the language and did not mention anything about the editing.

At this stage the book was sent for editing. The person chosen for this purpose was someone who had worked for the Hindustan Times. I had a few sittings with him before he started the work of editing. He was very serious about his work and took great pains in doing his job. When the manuscript was returned to me by him, I found it so much corrected that for a moment I was stunned. I could not believe that my language required that much correction. I was also not sure whether the edited draft carried the same meaning I intended to convey.

I discussed the matter with my wife who also felt the same way. Then the thought came to my mind that I should carefully go through the corrected draft and I did so patiently. I noticed that the corrected draft was much better though here and there it also changed the original intentions, therefore, decided to moderate it further and to come up with something in between. My publisher also advised me to do the same. As a result, the whole exercise was carried out again and I had to rewrite the whole thing in the light of the editor's correction. The final draft, which came out as a result of this exercise, turned out to be much better both in terms of precision and content. The editor himself was quite happy and approved it for publication.

The lesson learnt from this incident is that there is always scope for improvement in whatever we think or do. Most of us resist the idea of being corrected by others and it creates great disharmony in our lives. The fact is that we are not able to see ourselves in an objective manner, something which is possible only by our well-wishers. Their advice should therefore be taken in the right spirit. If we do so, our lives will turn out to be much more beautiful and harmonious. Someone has rightly said that the biggest room in this world is the room for improvement. Saint Kabir also meant the same thing when he said :

बुरा जो देखन मैं चला, बुरा न मिलियो कोय।
जो दिल खोजा आपनो, मुझसे बुरा न कोय॥

What can be a better lesson for self-improvement !

> *When you are angry ....*
>
> *You lose more than your temper !*
>
> *Always Remember !*
>
> *Anger is just a 'D' short of Danger !*

34

STATE OF FLUX

Evils prevailing in the society upset most of us and we keep wondering whether a time would ever come when there would be no evil. Some of us even try to reduce, remove or eradicate the evil. Many also regretfully compare the present with the past and worry about the future. Their concern is to be well appreciated, but the situation has to be seen more objectively.

I am of the view that the society has never been free from evil though the form of evil keeps changing with time. When we read history, we find that many evils which do not exist today existed in the past and the reverse is also true, as today we see many evils which were non-existent in the past. Similarly, in today's society, there are many good things which were non-existent in the past.

Thus, evil and good are only an indication of negative and positive tendencies. They both have to coexist though their form and effect may change with time. Everything will come to a standstill if either of them is missing. A battery needs both positive and negative terminals if the current has to flow. Similarly, the whole dynamics of the society will come to a halt if any of its components is missing. The situation can be compared with the 'state of flux' which is a continuous beam consisting of positive, negative and neutral particles. Both goodness and evil have a role to play. It is, therefore, pointless to think of a society which is totally free of evil.

The world will not change. You have to change yourself.

35

LIVING IN THE PRESENT

In one book of the Dalai Lama, I got a very interesting interpretation of the 'present'. We are generally advised to live in the present. This is so, because the past has gone and we can do nothing about it while the future is yet to come and is unknown, so why should we worry about it ? Therefore, we should look at the present only so that we make the best and optimum use of our energy and efforts. This approach also helps us to insulate ourselves from the regrets of the past and the worries of the future.

While explaining this concept, the Dalai Lama has tried to define the 'present'. He says that the moment we think of the present, it becomes the past and if we think about a point in time even slightly ahead, it is the future. The difference can be reduced to infinitely small units, as small as in nano-seconds or even less. Going by this logic, there is nothing like the 'present'. It is like a 'Point' in geometry which is defined as something which has no length or breadth. The moment we make a point it acquires both qualities. Similarly, with the 'present', the moment we try to catch it, it becomes either the past or the future.

This being so, 'living in the present' loses its meaning in the literal sense. It only means 'living beyond time' or in 'timelessness', thus caring neither for the past nor the future, nor even the present. It also means living at the level of consciousness which is beyond time. One may also call it the 'spiritual concept of time'. Perhaps, the advice to live in the present is only a simple way of advising people to live in consciousness, in order to raise themselves from the worries of the past, present and future.

> The 'present' is the only time, when we can work and achieve.

36
WOMEN AND GOLD

The Gospels of Swami Ramakrishna Paramahansa is the detailed record of informal conversations Swamiji used to have with the visitors to the Dakshineshwar temple. This work was very elaborately compiled by one of his close disciples. The original work was in Bengali and was subsequently translated and published in two volumes by the Ramakrishna Mission. They make very lucid reading and give in depth, the philosophy of Sri Ramakrishna through informal chats. While posted at Calcutta, I got these volumes and went through them.

One of the commonly used phrases in these volumes is 'Women and Gold'. Swamiji often used to advise his visitors to shun both of them. According to him, these two are the main causes of man's downfall. Those who did not understand the significance of these two words and took them literally were often wonderstruck. They could not think of giving up their wealth or wife and many even stopped visiting him on this account. Those who understood the true import of these words were greatly benefited.

Here the two words indicate two tendencies, namely 'lust' and 'greed'. Woman is a symbol of 'lust' while 'gold' is that of 'greed'. These two are the main weaknesses of man and are responsible for his downfall. Therefore, there is a need to guard oneself from them, though not necessarily to shun them. Lust and greed have to be shunned and once we do it, both of them can be useful instruments in our inner growth. This is what Sri

Ramakrishna meant while warning against 'Women and Gold'. In fact, the word used by him was '*Kamini Kanchan*', a literal translation meaning 'Woman and Gold.'

Here a clarification is necessary, as some may draw an inference that the woman is being looked down upon. This is not true, even remotely. Hinduism, in particular, has given a very high place to women. It is only when a woman becomes an object of lust that the society gets degenerated. This is very evident in today's context when lust for women has given rise to many social evils. Swami Ramakrishna meant only to warn against this fact.

> *The country and that nation which do not respect women have never become great nor will even be in future.*
>
> *Wealth consists not in having great possession, but in having few wants.*

37

COCONUT WATER

Much is said about 'gratefulness'. To be happy we should not expect anything in return for good done by us to others while we should always be grateful for whatever good has been done to us by others. It does not mean that goodness is not returned by goodness but that such an attitude insulates us from agony of disappointment, if this does not happen. Secondly, the laws of nature are perfect. Here, goodness never goes unrewarded while the evil never remains unpunished. It being so, why should we waste our energy in keeping account of our goodness ? Quite often, our goodness is returned to us through unknown sources and in the same way evil is also returned. Therefore, we should confine ourselves to doing good deeds while being grateful for every good act done to us.

Here, the example of a coconut tree is most appropriate. A coconut plant needs watering and care for the initial two years. Then it takes care of itself and grows into a tree. Once it starts giving fruits, it continues to do so for more than fifty years and needs no watering. All the water given to it in the first two years is returned by it manifold in the form of coconut water. Such should be our attitude towards those who do good to us. Every little helpful deed, kind word or thoughtful gesture should be gratefully remembered and returned to the extent possible. Once we start doing so, our happiness multiplies and so do our friends.

> He who receives a benefit should never forget it; he who bestows should never remember it.

38
KNOWLEDGE AND WISDOM

We often fail to draw a distinction between knowledge and wisdom. This leads to conflicts in many areas. The conflict between generations is mainly due to the lack of appreciation of this difference. At times our knowledge says something but the experience says something else. Those who understand the difference are able to harmonise the conflict while those who do not, lose their peace of mind. An effort is, therefore, being made to clarify the difference between 'knowledge' and 'wisdom' in a simple manner.

Wallace Friday has said, "Real Wisdom is more than Knowledge. Knowledge is the accumulation of facts; Wisdom is the interpretation of facts. Knowledge is culled from textbooks; Wisdom comes out of life."

This quotation makes the distinction very clear. Wisdom comes by living well, by contemplation and by inculcating values in life. Knowledge can be acquired in a short time, but wisdom is acquired with time. Knowledge is no guarantee of success and harmony in life but a wise person is always successful and in tune with himself and the world. A Knowledgeable person may be literate but not educated, while a wise person is always educated. Knowledge is like 'science' while wisdom is like 'technology' which is applied science. As technology is more useful to mankind, so is the wise person as compared to the knowledgeable. Knowledge is only one component of wisdom, though an important one.

Having understood the difference, we must strive to grow wise. Then only will our value system become our asset and our lives become successful and harmonious. If we commit the mistake of taking 'knowledge' as a complete strategy in itself, we are in for trouble. No purpose will then be served by blaming the world around. On the other hand, a wise person has no complaint. For him, all situations are the varieties of life and he enjoys them all.

> Real Optimism is aware of problems....
> but recognises the solutions....
> knows about difficulties....
> but believes they can be overcome....
> sees the negative, but accentuates the positive....
> is exposed to the worst, but expects the best....
> has reason to complain, but chooses to smile !
>
> *William Arthur Ward*

39

LIFE BEFORE DEATH

Human life is the most precious thing in this universe. Also, it is so complex that many have been studying its various facets since time immemorial. There is an ocean of wisdom dealing with human life but still there is very little known about it. Perception about human life differs from person to person and they live according to their individual perception. In a way, this makes the world a beautiful place to live in by the sheer variety of human beings. A truly wise person accepts this variety with equanimity and considers it as a part of the evolution process.

One interesting aspect of life which is usually debated is 'what happens after death'. Hindu philosophy believes in the theory of rebirth while there are some which do not believe in rebirth. I am not going into the merits of such belief or disbelief but am touching upon an allied aspect of this.

Recently I read a book called *Dewdrops on a Lotus Leaf,* a very interesting book written by a young professor of English in Andhra Pradesh. The book consists of letters written by the author to his loved ones on different occasions. Each letter is full of wisdom and indicates the spiritual depth of the author.

In one of the letters, the question of life after death has been raised. The author has said nothing about his belief in this matter but has seen the issue from a totally different viewpoint. I greatly appreciated his approach and am sharing it here.

The author mentions that many people ask him the question, "Is there life after death?" and instead of giving any reply, he poses a counter-question, "Is there life before death?" Now the significance of such a response is to be understood carefully. The issue here is which of the two, 'life after death' or 'life before death', is more important. Naturally, the answer would be that 'life before death' is more important and we should first live it well before we think of 'life after death'. The intention is not to curb the tendency to question but to give a positive message about the life we already have.

In today's world, most of us are not living even in our present lives. We waste time on trivials without caring about the precious nature of life. For such persons, the question of whether there is life after death is meaningless because they are dead even in their lives before death. The relevant question, therefore, is how to live before death. And if we really live well before death, perhaps, there will be no life after death. Thus, in both the situations, the question 'Is there life after death?' becomes irrelevant. The only relevant question is whether our 'Life before Death' is 'living' in the true sense as morally and spiritually enriched human beings, well on the way to the goal of self-realisation and harmony with oneself, other people and the universe.

> You only live once, but if you live right,
> once is enough.

40

ROLE OF THE WICKED

Sri Ramakrishna lived at a time when theatres were very popular in Bengal. Sometimes, Sri Ramakrishna himself used to visit them at the request of his devotees. Many of his devotees were connected with theatres as owners, actors or participants in allied activities. At Dakshineswar, in the company of devotees, the master often talked about theatres and drew many deep spiritual lessons from them. One such lesson was about the "role of the wicked".

Many visitors to Dakshineswar used to ask Sri Ramakrishna about the evils prevailing in the society and the purpose served by them. Some of the devotees were themselves not very pious persons and indulged in all sorts of worldly activities. However, those who continued to live in the company of the master grew fast and triumphed over their weaknesses. Those who did not, left his company and returned to their old ways. Swamiji was never upset at such happenings and gave full freedom to his devotees to choose their path. He confined himself only to revealing truth. Fortunate ones grasped it while others only laughed. He accepted both the responses with equanimity.

Whenever asked about the role of evil or the wicked, Sri Ramakrishna gave the example of a play on the stage of the theatre. According to him we all are actors on this worldly stage. Like a stage drama, we all play different roles on earth and once the drama is over, we return to our permanent abode. In a drama there are all types of roles. Someone plays the role of a hero and the other plays the role of villain. Both roles are equally important and the success of the drama depends upon both. The drama will lose all its charm if any one of them is absent.

The same is the case with the worldly drama also. Here, all kinds of people are required to make it dynamic and interesting. If we look at evil and wickedness from this viewpoint, all our fear, hatred or complaints against them will disappear. Instead, we shall have harmony with them also. Not only this, when seen this way, we shall find their roles as important as those of good persons.

This is how Sri Ramakrishna explained the 'role of the wicked".

The Treasures of Time

*Yesterday is but
a dream
and Tomorrow is
only a vision.*

*But Today, well
lived...
makes every Yesterday
a dream of happiness...*

*and every Tomorrow
a vision of hope !*

41
ALL THINGS ARE SMALL

Our scriptures teach us to live in this world in a detached manner. If we are fortunate enough to imbibe this in our lives, we make ourselves happy and little things do not bother us. The greater the degree of detachment, the greater is our capacity to accept things as they are and the greater is our peace of mind. Now the question is, what things should bother us and what not ? The answer to this is not easy and varies from person to person. A thing which is insignificant for one may not be so for the other. However, a general principle may apply to all. I learnt this from a real-life episode which was narrated during a training programme which I am sharing here.

There was a famous cardiologist in the US, who was a very busy person. Apart from being occupied in his medical practice, he rushed to various cities to deliver lectures on his subject. All his lectures drew huge crowds and this made him all the more popular and busy. His schedule, therefore, had become so hectic that his health came under great strain.

Once he flew to a place to deliver a lecture but just before reaching the venue, he suffered a heart attack and was rushed to a hospital. Fortunately, he was attended to quickly and his life was saved. He recovered and went to deliver the lecture on the very next day. The news of his heart attack was kept a secret by his managers and so the audience was waiting eagerly for his talk.

This time his lecture was altogether different. He did not speak on the complex systems of the heart and the human body and the complicated ways of keeping them healthy. Instead, he said that human life was very precious and should not be wasted on trivial things. Defining what these small things were, the exact words he used were:

Small things are not worth dying for;
And all things are small.

He concluded his lecture with these few lines, pleading that this formula was enough to keep the heart and body healthy.

I consider that his advice advocated nothing but the principle of detachment. Life is too precious to be wasted on small things, and all worldly things are small when compared to the real goal of life.

> All are architects of Fate,
> Working in these walls of Time,
>
> For the structures that we raise,
> Time is with materials filled.
>
> Our todays and yesterday,
> Are the blocks with which we build,
>
> Build today, then, strong and sure,
> With a firm and ample base,
>
> And ascending and secure,
> Shall tomorrow find its place.
>
> *Henry W. Longfellow*

42

STRENGTH OF HUMILITY

Humility is often a misunderstood word. Many confuse it with meekness or weakness. The result is that they resort to arrogance and waste a lot of energy in the process. This is very unfortunate. Therefore, the need is to understand the word 'humility' carefully. While the outer manifestations of 'humility' and 'meekness' may be the same, the inner situation is totally different. Humility can be shown only by a strong, fearless and a detached person while meekness is the result of weakness, fear or undue expectation. Humility is an ornament of the brave while meekness is a symptom of cowardice. Once we understand this difference well, we can cultivate humility in a natural manner, thus conserving our energy which can be used for more constructive purposes.

I learnt the above lesson from a book on Lal Bahadur Shastri written by an ex-director of the Lal Bahadur Shastri National Academy of Administration, Mussoorie. He was also my Director when I was there for the IAS training course. He had worked with Shastriji for a long time and had known him closely. He also used to deliver a few lectures on the personality of Shastriji to the probationers. I was greatly influenced by his lectures as well as the book.

Shastriji came from a background of penury but rose to the position of the Prime Minister of India. All through he was a humble but in no way a weak man. He had the courage to own responsibility for mistakes committed by his subordinates and also the nerve to take strong decisions whenever necessary. This was amply evident during the Indo-Pak war of 1965. Even in Tashkent, he had displayed tremendous courage during the talks with Ayub Khan when he refused to budge from his stand on Kashmir. He lived a very simple life and commanded the respect of all. When he gave a call to give up cereals once a week, the whole nation responded positively because of the respect he commanded.

Who says that humility is weakness? Only those who are humble in the true sense enjoy the strength of humility.

> We do not count a man's years,
> until he has nothing else to count.
>
> Age is quality of mind,
> If you have left your dreams behind,
> If hope is cold,
> If you no longer look ahead,
> If your ambition's fires are dead....
> Then you are old !
>
> But if from life you take the best,
> And if in life you keep the zest,
> If love you hold.
> No matter how the years go by,
> No matter how the birthdays fly...
> You are not old !

43

POWER OF COMPASSION

The Dalai Lama, the spiritual and the political head of Tibet, has lived a long life in exile, struggling for the rights of his people. An ordinary mortal would have broken down in such a situation, which, perhaps, would have brought more misery and indignity to his people. He, however, by his wisdom and moral strength has not only been struggling for them but has also maintained their dignity. He has won the 'Nobel Peace Prize' which speaks volumes about him.

I have read the Dalai Lama's autobiography, *Freedom in Exile*. It gives a detailed account of the situation in Tibet which led to his exile and the troubles as well as indignities thrust upon him and his people. However, in the midst of all this, he kept his composure and led his people with dignity. It was not an easy task and he explains it in another book, *The Power of Compassion*. While describing the agonies of his life, he writes that it was the power of compassion which helped him greatly in maintaining his peace of mind and in following the path of wisdom. I am sharing here a lesson learnt from this book.

First of all the word 'compassion' should be understood clearly. This word has a unique meaning and is different from mercy. In fact, it is more than mercy. It is putting oneself in the position of a suffering person and feeling exactly what he does. It is closer to the word 'empathy' which means the power of entering into another's personality and experiencing his experiences. When one has compassion for others, one has great magnetic power and even an enemy can be won over by the power of compassion.

This is exactly true in the case of Dalai Lama. He has not only been able to win his people by his compassion, but has also dealt with his enemies in a dignified manner. This in turn greatly helped his cause and won worldwide concern about it.

Once we understand the power of compassion, it can be used as a tool to deal with others. By compassion, we win not only our friends and well-wishers but our enemies too. Our apparently harsh actions are then seen as kind deeds, and harmony comes to our life naturally.

Life gives what you ask !

I bargained with Life for a penny,
    And Life would pay no more;
However I begged at evening,
    When I counted my scanty store.

For Life is a just employer,
    He gives you what you ask;
But once you have set the wages,
    Then, you must bear the task.

I worked for a menial's hire,
    Only to learn, dismayed,
That my wage I had asked of Life,
    Life would have willingly paid.

Jessie Rittenhouse

44

VARIETY NOT HIERARCHY

All of us see so much disparity in this world that at times one doubts the fairness of God. Quite a few of us do not believe in God merely for this reason. However, it is not fair to pass judgement on the fairness of God without going deeper into the matter. I read a book which explained this disparity in a very convincing manner, helping me to see the light.

The author says that God does not have any bias while creating a particular thing or situation. He creates with objectivity and the idea of disparity does not even come into His mind. For God, everything is a variety and not a hierarchy. It is man who creates a hierarchy and makes God responsible for it. Thus, when we see a rich and a poor person, both are two varieties of God. From God's viewpoint, no hierarchy is attached to them. Seen from the worldly angle it is true that richness has its own blessings as well as troubles and just as poverty also has. The same axiom applies to the beautiful and the ugly, the strong and the weak, the pious and the wicked, the high and the low, the healthy and the unhealthy.

When we see the world around us with such an attitude of acceptance, it appears beautiful to us and nothing creates disharmony. We accept it as such while trying our best to improve it. It then becomes like a garden which has a variety of flowers, trees and fruits. The different colours of flowers, the varied shapes of the trees and the different tastes of fruits only add to the charm of the garden. As it would not be fair to create a hierarchy among them, so is it true with the world also. Instead, the disparities should be appreciated as the multifaceted aspects of life and not as higher or lower, better or worse.

45

ANSWERS OF OUR PROBLEMS

Life is like a book of mathematics. There are many chapters in it and as we go to higher classes the lessons become more complicated. If we fail to understand the principles right in the beginning, the lessons appear more complicated. In all the chapters, the principles are explained first and then some solved examples are given. After understanding both, we are supposed to solve unsolved problems. The real test of our knowledge comes there. Based upon our understanding of the principles and the solved examples given in the book we are able to tackle the sums. Every problem has a solution and there is a definite answer for each. The only difficulty is that we may not know them though they are given at the back of the book.

The same is true with life. What we learn from the book of life and its solved problems is to be used for handling many unexpected and troubling situations. If lessons from the book of life are not understood properly or we are not attentive while our problems are being solved by others, we find life miserable and all its problems remain as they are. We then start blaming the world instead of enjoying it. If, on the other hand, we carefully understand the principles of life and apply them to real-life problems, life becomes enjoyable and enriching. Each problem of life has a solution and an answer. It is a different matter that we may not know it. God only hides it till the end of the book of life.

Let us, therefore, not consider that our problems do not have a solution. If the solution is given to us by someone else, the whole charm of life will go. There may not be an immediate answer to some problems but the answer definitely exists, and it may only take a little longer to reach them. Maybe, we have to learn how to read the book of life better.

46

THE ENTROPY LAW

We all know that the society has passed through its four stages of Satyuga, Tretayuga, Dwaparyuga and Kaliyuga. At present we are in Kaliyuga and it is said that even this stage is reaching its last phase. The present is considered bad because the evils in society have assumed gigantic proportions and there are very few who think of the larger good. Most people have become selfish and think only of themselves. The result is that society is in a hellish state and nobody knows how to come out of this chaos. We also hear that the situation was most ideal in Satyuga but then deteriorated over the centuries. Thus values have fallen with time. Dwaparyuga was better than Kaliyuga, Tretayuga was better than Dwaparyuga and Satyuga was better than Tretayuga. I have been thinking about the reasons for this fall in values and was seeking a scientific explanation of this phenomenon when I found a book which gave me the answer which tallied with my own intuition.

The above phenomenon is explained by the second law of thermodynamics. There are two laws of thermodynamics. The first one is the 'law of conservation' which says that energy can neither be created nor destroyed but can only be transformed from one form to another. The second law of thermodynamics says that every time energy is transformed from one state to another, there is a loss in the amount of that form of energy which then becomes available to perform work of some kind. This loss in the amount of 'available energy' is known as 'entropy'. For example, if we burn a piece of coal, the total amount of energy remains the same but, due to the process of burning, some part of the coal is transformed into sulphur dioxide and cannot be reburnt to get the same work out of it. This kind of 'loss', 'wastage' or 'penalty' is called entropy.

The second law of thermodynamics explains that the total entropy in the world is constantly increasing. An entropy increase, therefore, means a decrease in 'available energy'. Further, not only does the available energy decrease everytime something occurs in this world but the unavailable energy spreads as pollution. Thus, the world is moving towards a dissipated state and pollution is constantly increasing.

Now, this has very great implications for the society. In practical terms, it means that the society deteriorates and becomes disorganised gradually. There is a degeneration in its moral force, its spiritual stamina, the vigour of its character, the effectiveness of its religion and the sense of law and order. Thus the moral and spiritual energy of the society goes on degenerating so that, ultimately, it reaches a stage of maximum entropy when God has to intervene. The trend has to be reversed to bring about Satyuga or Golden Age when all material things have maximum energy concentration, i.e., are Satopradhan and the souls also have maximum 'available' moral and spiritual energy. The process of degeneration then begins again and the cycle goes on. The need for God's action in such a situation is evident because, according to the entropy law, in a closed system, entropy increase cannot be reversed without increasing the entropy in the surroundings and, therefore an outside source of energy is required to raise the energy concentration without lowering the energy level in the surroundings.

Thus the 'entropy law' explains the degenerative process of the society. This is a natural process and need not unduly upset us. The only option we have is to mould ourselves into a closed system so that our own entropy does not increase and our moral and spiritual stamina is maintained. As far as the whole or universal system is concerned, God will take care of it at the appropriate time. Therefore, it has been rightly suggested that we should live in the world but the world should not live in us.

> Understand what this world is,
> so that it may not hurt you.

47
THE PHOTOGRAPH HAS CHANGED

I belong to a town in district Muzaffarnagar of U.P. After initial education in my home town, I studied there for five years before going to Roorkee University for my Engineering degree. Fortunately I have kept myself in touch with all these places and frequently visit them. As a result I have a good number of friends and well-wishers at all these places.

As is its nature, life has seen lot of changes during this period. Perhaps it has been more so in my case. After passing engineering, I did not stay in that profession for long and shifted to Indian Administration Service. In this service also I was assigned U.P. cadre which provided me opportunity to visit my home town and the district frequently. I also developed interest in the spiritual aspect of life and its relevance to day-to-day life. This made me to think deeper and I started interpreting day-to-day event from spiritual viewpoint. Soon these thoughts took the shape of books which draw attention of many. This also became helpful in adding my friends and well-wishers.

One such addition is in the form of a group at Muzaffarnagar consisting mostly of local doctors. All of them are not only successful in the career but are also blessed with the quest of seeking truth. This common interest brought us together and whenever occasion comes we meet to share our views. It is always an elevating experience and greatly helps me in contemplation.

During one of such interaction a very interesting observation was made by one of the participant. Two of my books had different photograph at the back cover. There was a gap of about eight years between them and naturally they appeared different. Noticing this difference, he made a very natural observation saying "Your photograph has changed." Somehow this phrase drew my deeper attention and we shifted our discussion to this interesting aspect of life.

We all know that out photograph is only a sketch of our outer personality and that too of only the body. The body keeps changing every moment but the change is so slow that we hardly notice it. Only over a period of time, these changes of body are noticed and a day comes when it totally vanishes. However, all through this period from birth to death, there is something which is permanent and does not change. That is why we always address ourselves as 'I'. Most of us waste our time and energy only on the vanishing part of our existence that is the body. Only fortunate few pay attention to the permanent part which is beyond bodily existence. Once our quest is directed to this aspect of the personality, all conflicts which belong only to the body start disappearing and we reach the state of bliss in increasing manner. Greater is the quest and effort, greater will be the achievement in this direction. We then rise above the changes of the body which in any case has to undergo this process. If so, why not to spend our energy on the development of our inner personality which gets refined with time, contrary to the outer personality which diminishes with time despite all our efforts. This is what is known as spiritual search or the process of self-realisation. Once on this path, photograph changes cease to be the cause of worry and we make best use of our energy both physical as well as spiritual.

> It would be much worse....
> to have perfect sight and no vision,
> than the other way around !
>
> *Helen Keller*

48
GURU POORNIMA

I was in the holy company of my spiritual master Swami Bhoomananda Tirtha on the auspicious occasion of 'Guru-Poornima' on 5th July, 2001 at 'NARAYANASHRAMA TAPOVANAM' in Trichur (Kerala). Every year, on this occasion, close devotees of Swamiji assemble in the ashram and spend about a week in his holy company. The first time, I attended this spiritual retreat, was in July, 1994 and thereafter it was my second visit during 'Guru Poornima'. This is a very sublime occasion and in India the tradition of 'Master-Disciple' meet on this day has been a long one. This is a time when a devotee assesses his progress on the path of spiritual journey and seeks necessary guidance from his master individually as well as collectively. On this day, after the worship of the guru, a message is given by him to his disciples. The message is always deep and helps a lot for further progress. I am hereby giving the extract of my masters message on this Guru Poornima, pointwise and in brief.

1. We should always keep in mind that we are not body. Body is mortal but we are not. This thought alone can take us to the pedestal of wisdom and our life can become truly fulfilled.
2. Only our 'Guru' can address us as immortal and no one else including the parents and school teachers. Guru sees the immortal in us and can make us feel immortal.
3. The truth of our being immortal was discovered countless generations ago and will remain so for countless generations. This is the true spiritual wisdom.

4. All wealth perishes but the wealth of spiritual wisdom does not and lives from generation to generation. Only if we are able to realise this truth in life, life becomes meaningful.
5. This knowledge is the key to all problems of life and changes its course for the better. In fact, this alone is the central message of Bhagvad Gita.
6. We should remember that destruction is never in the nature of nature. Nature only knows transformation and evolution. This being so, whatever happens in life should be welcome.
7. Spiritual infection has to begin in everyone's life some day or the other. This call of spirituality is the most important call of life. Fortunate are those in whose life this call comes early.
8. Guru Poornima is an occasion to assess our progress and make necessary correction or modification in the journey of spiritual progress.
9. Loss and gain both are parts of life. Take them as they come. The fact is that we learn more from the loss than from gain. Also, ultimately all that is mundane is to perish. Then why to grieve on loss or hail the gain.
10. Our suffering is on account of cause and effect. There is no option to it except to exhaust it. Tragedies of life are not to be ignored or laughed upon, they are to be endured.
11. We should take necessary care of body. It should be fed, clothed and kept appropriately. All this should never mean that we become the body and neglect the immortal part of us.
12. Desire, fear, greed, and all other negative impulses are part of life. They have to be understood well and transcended. Once we understand their genesis, the transcendence becomes easy.
13. 'Guru-shishya' relationship should grow with time. It is a very precious association. A shishya is a member of guru's family.
14. All duties carried out with devotion is a part of divine service and a step towards spiritual progress. The purpose

of each activity is to dissolve ego and become weightless. This is the essence of entire spirituality.
15. Progress in spiritual path means expansion of mind so that the entire creation of God appears as one family. Guru helps in such an expansion of mind. Once this happens, realisation of our immorality is a natural outcome.

With this message Swamiji blessed all the devotees.

> To live content with small means...
> To seek elegance, rather than luxury...
> And refinement, rather than fashion....
> To be worthy, not respectable....
> And wealthy, not rich...
>
> To study hard, think quietly...
> Talk gently, act frankly...
> To liten to stars and birds....
> Babes and sages, with open heart...
> To bear all cheerfully....
> And do all bravely....
>
> This is my vision of life !
>
> **William Channing**

49

GOD AND THE GOVERNMENT

For all rational people, God is the greatest mystery despite the fact that He is said to be omnipotent and omnipresent. It is also said that God is present in all things sentient as well as non-sentient. If it is so what is His form and where does He live? This is a question which comes and should come to every thinking mind. Most of us accept God in the form, our mind has been trained to believe by our observation of family and social traditions. Some form their opinion by the study of books both authentic and not so authentic. No wonder God is conceived in different forms by different people resulting into more and more confusion. I have myself been quite confused about the concept of God and have contemplated a lot on the subject. In this brief write up I am trying to narrate the outcome of my contemplation on God.

In India, most of the people still believe in personal Gods. For them God has a definite form either human or non-human. They believe that God is a kind of super ruler and behaves that way. He has the power of rewarding as well as punishing. People also believe that God can be pleased by their external acts and in order to seek His blessing they indulge in all sorts of rituals. If their wishes are granted fully or partially they feel that the God is kind and just. But if their wishes are not granted despite their rituals, they even call Him cruel and unjust. Those who think rationally refuse to accept such an arbitrary God and in the process stop believing in the existence of God itself. I feel that this write up may be helpful for them though I also feel that many such rational people must have their own concept of God. The problem is further compounded by the fact that God is invisible through external senses and any discussion about Him can only be appreciated at level higher than that of senses. With this background let me speak about my concept of God.

According to me God is akin to a government. As a government runs the administration of a country or a province or a district, in the same way God also runs the administration of the universe. We must appreciate that there are laws of universe which have to be followed or complied with properly. If it is not so there shall be greater disorder and the living will become impossible. There has to be some power which must be controlling all these laws of the universe. I feel that God is this power and that is why it is called omnipotent. However, here omnipotent does not mean to be arbitary. Such a great power like God can never be arbitrary. God's purpose is to ensure that universal laws are followed by everyone and if there is any defaults, corrective action is taken accordingly. We may call such actions by any name like punishment or cruelty but God does not inflict them with any such intention. He only ensures the enforcement of laws in order to run the Universe. Similarly there is no such thing as reward and everyone only reaps the fruits of his or her actions. This way God is the most neutral entity which neither distributes any awards or inflicts any punishment but only ensures that everyone gets his due. There may be phase difference between our timings and His timings and that is why at times there is delay in the system of awards or punishments. Some of us may interpret it as God's injustice or arbitrariness but the fact is that virtue is always rewarded and evil is always punished. While there may be exceptions and failures in the system of human Government, there is no such chance in God's Government. Thus while God is all powerful, His exercise of power is governed by fixed universal laws and there can be no arbitrariness. This way God is very much like an ideal government, which is supposed to make laws and ensure their compliance in order to run the society smoothly.

Now we come to the omnipresence and invisibility of the God. For this also we have to understand the nature of the government. After all whom do we call government in a geographical unit be it a country, a province or a district? If we think deeply no single person can be called Government and whosoever is carrying out the function of the Government, he or she is the government at that place. It may be a minister, a collector, a police official, a tax official, a peon or any other functionary of the government. While the nature of their jobs or level of powers may vary, but all of them perform the duty of the government at their respective places. This way government instead of being concentrated in a single person is spread in all its constituents. This is not the case only with sentient constituents, it is so with non-sentient components also. That is why a vehicle, a piece of furniture and all the articles belonging to a Government office also become part of the government. Seen this way, government is something which is manifested in all its constituents while as a single entity it is always invisible.

The same thing applies to God. God being the Government of the universe is also manifested through all its creation sentient as well as non-sentient. Whatever God does is through its constituents only. When God helps someone, He does so through some of its creature and also when He punishes some of us, He does so through some different creature. Thus the whole system of creation is so interwoven that each of the units carries out the function of God only. This is perhaps each creation is said to be a part of God only and one who sees God in all is godly in true sense. This way God is nothing but the sum total of the creation and that is why it is called "Paramatma" while its constituents are called "Atmas". Since the creation of God is present everywhere, God is also omnipresent. Also God is so subtly present in its creation that it is not possible to see or experience Him easily. That is why it is invisible to most of us.

Somehow I find that this explanation of God clarifies all possible doubts about Him. Hence I am sharing it with others. However, everyone is entitled to his or her own version of God.

Surely it does not affect the reality and God will continue to be what It is. To me it only shows that God is really incomprehensive for little minds like us and even we all together fail to describe God in totality.

50

WHO NEEDS GOD ?

I am closing this book with this lesson. Many years ago, I read a book titled *Who Needs God?* written by Harold Kushner, the author of a famous book called *When Bad Things Happen to Good People*. Since then I have been contemplating over the subject deeply, but frankly speaking, the true concept of God is still not clear to me. I think that it is a mystery for most. Everyone has his own perception of God and proceeds from there. Perhaps, God is not comprehensible for mortals like us. All my contemplation has led me to believe that there is a higher being like God whom we need sometime or the other. Even those who deny the existence of God think of Him, though in a different form. I shall try to give an answer to the question 'Who Needs God?' and for this I quote a portion of the introduction from the book which goes like this :

"I deal with bright, successful people, people I genuinely like and admire, and I sense that something is missing in their lives. There is a lack of rootedness, a sense of having to figure things out by themselves because the past cannot be trusted as their guide. Their celebrations, from their children's birthday parties to a daughter's wedding to a business milestone, can be lots of fun but rarely soar to the level of joy. And as they grow older, I suspect they either confront or actively hide from confronting the thought that 'there must be more to life than this.'

"There is a spiritual vacuum at the centre of their lives, and their lives betray this lack of an organising vision, a sense of 'this is who I am and what my life is fundamentally about.' Some look for that centre in their work, and are disappointed when corporations choose not to repay the loyalty they demanded or when retirement leaves them, feeling useless. Some try to find it in their families, and don't understand why they are so hurt when adolescent children insist, 'Let me lead my own life!' and adult children move to another state and call every other Sunday. And for some reason, it never occurs to them to ask, 'How did previous generations find meaning in their lives?'

"For almost thirty years, I have tried to show my congregants how much more fulfilled they would be if they made room for their religious tradition in their lives. I have urged them to do it, not to make God happy but to make themselves happy. I have told them the Hassidic story of the man who got a telegram telling him that a relative had died and left him some valuable property. He was to contact the rabbi for details. Excited, he went to the rabbi, only to be told that the relative was Moses and the valuable property was the Jewish religious tradition. And much of the time, they reacted as I suspect the man in the story did, disappointed that their legacy was religious wisdom and not downtown real estate.

"This book is the product of those years of thinking and teaching on the issue of what we lose when we become too intellectual or too modern to make room for religion in our lives. It is about what has happened to the souls of modern men and women under the impact of modern life, what we have lost in the process of gaining personal freedom and material comfort. But more than that, it is the summary of what my own life has been about, what has gotten me through bad times and taught me how to celebrate the good times, how I have learned to recognise the extraordinary things that even the most ordinary lives contain.

"The thesis of this book is that there is a kind of nourishment our souls crave, even as our bodies need the right foods, sunshine, and exercise. Without that spiritual nourishment, our souls remain stunted and undeveloped. In the physical realm, we understand that our ancestors' hard physical work built muscles and burned off calories, but today we are the victims of a modern lifestyle, so we need to diet, to jog, to work out at the gym. So, too, the kind of spiritual communion our forebears knew is less accessible to us because the world is so noisy and full of distractions, because we are so dazzled by our power and success, because religion in the late twentieth century is often badly packaged or presented by people we cannot trust or admire."

I feel that this extract is enough to convey my message. We all have some vacuum in our lives, howsoever fulfilled we may feel. It is only God who can fill this vacuum and make our lives meaningful. It is a different matter that some of us may fail to see or pretend not to see the vacuum, but all of us do need God.

If man unbuilded goes !

We are all blind until we see
What is the human plan ?
Nothing is worth the making if
It does not make the man.

Why build these cities glorious
If man unbuilded goes ?
In vain we build the work, unless
The Builder also grows.

Edwin Markham

THE GOAL OF LIFE

O man! The Goal Of life is God-realisation.

God-realisation grants Supreme Joy, Peace and Fearlessness. Most precious is human birth. Utilise this birth to attain God. Life is short. Time is fleeting. Waste not time. Engage in noble deeds. Be up and doing upon the path of Divine Life.

Serve, Love, Give, Purify, Meditate, Realise. Be good; do good. Be kind; be compassionate. Practise non-injury, truth and purity. This is the foundation of Yoga and Vedanta. Adapt, adjust, accommodate. Bear insult; bear injury. Serve all. Love all, Embrace all in the Oneness of the Spirit. This is divine life.

Enquire 'Who am I ?' Know thy Self and be free. Thou art not this body, not this mind. Thou art Immortal Self. Thou art unborn, eternal, changeless, indestructible, ever pure, all-perfect Spirit or Atman. Realise this and be free. This is your foremost duty. Do this through selflessness and service, devotion and worship, purification, concentration and meditation. Attain God-realisation. Do it now. Abide in Bliss, Peace and Perfection for ever.

— *Swami Sivananda*